New Covenant Prophetic Ministry

Jim & Carolyn Welton

New Covenant Prophetic Ministry
Copyright © 2014—Carolyn Welton & Jim Welton

All rights reserved. This book is protected by the copyright laws of the United States of America. This book may not be copied or reprinted for commercial gain or profit. The use of short quotations or occasional page copying for personal or group study is permitted and encouraged. Permission will be granted upon request.

Unless otherwise identified, Scripture quotations are taken from the THE HOLY BIBLE, NEW INTERNATIONAL VERSION®, NIV®. Copyright © 1973, 1978, 1984, 2010 by Biblica, Inc.™ www.xulonpress.com.

Scripture quotations marked NKJV are taken from the New King James Version. Copyright © 1982 by Thomas Nelson, Inc. Used by permission. All rights reserved. Scripture quotations marked KJV are taken from the King James Version.

ISBN   978-0-9905752-0-7

Contents

Foreword by Dr. Jonathan Welton...5
Introduction...9

one	In Defense of Prophecy...13
two	God's Word: An Anchor...19
three	Restoration: The Framework...27
four	The Prophetic Pyramid...35
five	The Revelation Gifts...53
six	Living in the Spirit Realm...63
seven	Rhythm and Rhyme...75
eight	Stewarding Your Personal Prophetic Words...85
nine	Fencing Out Deception...97
ten	Balaam and the False Prophets...107
eleven	The Character of the Servant of the Lord...125

Conclusion...133
Appendix: Forming Prophetic Teams...135
Endnotes...145

Foreword

Many bad prophets have existed throughout the history of the Church.

If books like the one you hold in your hands had existed, far fewer of these bad prophets would have existed. Now don't misunderstand me; I am not speaking about preventing cults and witchcraft. Obviously those are wrong. But a false prophet is not the same as a bad prophet. Bad prophets are trying their best, but they get things wrong; they are sometimes inaccurate and make mistakes.

In Deuteronomy 13 we see the definition of an actual *false prophet*:

> *If a prophet, or one who foretells by dreams, appears among you and announces to you a sign or wonder, and if the sign or wonder spoken of takes place, and the prophet says, "Let us follow other gods" (gods you have not known) "and let us worship them," you must not listen to the words of that prophet or dreamer. The Lord your God is testing you to find out whether you love him with all your heart and with all your soul. It is the Lord your God you must follow, and him you must revere. Keep his commands and obey him; serve him and hold fast to him* (Deuteronomy 13:1–4).

Here the false prophets actually got their predictions correct! What made them false was their intention to lead the people after false gods. False prophets are accurate, but they lead people down a path of destruction.

Later on in Deuteronomy 18, we meet the *bad prophet*:

> *I will raise up for them a prophet like you from among their fellow Israelites, and I will put my words in his mouth. He will tell them everything I command him. I myself will call to account anyone who does not listen to my words that the prophet speaks in my name. But a prophet who presumes to speak in my name anything I have not commanded, or a prophet who speaks in the name of other gods, is to be put to death. You may say to yourselves, "How can we know when a message has not been spoken by the Lord?" If what a prophet proclaims in the name of the LORD does not take place or come true, that is a message the LORD has not spoken. That prophet has spoken presumptuously; so do not be alarmed* (Deuteronomy 18:18–22).

We see in verse 18 that this type of prophet is raised up by God as His representative. But if such prophets speak presumptuously (from their own hearts, independent of God's direct revelation), the people will know they are wrong because their words won't come to pass. In Deuteronomy 13, the false prophet was accurate but led the people after false gods, whereas in chapter 18 the bad prophet was a true prophet of God who at times spoke presumptuously and inaccurately.

How are we to respond to these two types of prophets?

> **But a prophet who presumes to speak in my name anything I have not commanded, or a prophet who speaks in the name of other gods, is to be put to death.**...*If what a prophet proclaims in the name of the LORD does not take place or come true, that is a message the LORD has not spoken.* **That prophet has spoken presumptuously; so do not be alarmed** (Deuteronomy 18:20–22).

This verse shows us two different responses depending on the type of prophet.

- Bad prophets who speak presumptuously/inaccurately — Don't be alarmed.

- False prophets who mislead people after other gods — Put them to death.

The Bad Prophet: If true prophets of God are inaccurate, they have spoken presumptuously, and the people should not be alarmed. Essentially, that means they don't need to be afraid of him, but they also should take them less seriously when they prophesy. This should be our response to many of the prophets in the modern Church. If their track record for prophetic words is inaccurate, we shouldn't be so moved when they prophesy. If they say California is going to be judged by God and then judgment doesn't come, or if they declare financial investments that never turn up positive, it is irresponsible for us to continue to hold them in high regard. At least until they stop speaking presumptuously, we must not put so much weight on their words.

The False Prophet: False prophets are accurate, but they lead people after other gods (see Deut 13:1–4). The instruction to ancient Israel was to put them to death (see Deut. 18:20). Clearly, as we are not ancient Israel, this command no longer applies. Yet we can see the difference between the two types of prophets and the two different responses commanded to Israel.

The implications of this difference are significant. When people prophesy, they can be inaccurate without being false prophets! God *never* commanded death to His own prophets when they were inaccurate. So we do not have to be afraid of practicing prophecy and joyfully learning to hear God's voice for ourselves and others. Jesus said His sheep will hear His voice (see John 10:3), and as His sheep, this is our privilege and our joy.

Here's one final thought. Prophecy has never changed, but the covenants have changed. Prophets have always been God's covenant lawyers. Under the Old Covenant, they came as God's lawyers to prosecute His case against His covenant partner Israel. Now in the New Covenant, they are still God's covenant lawyers, but the covenant has changed. Instead of pointing out guilt, sin, and condemnation, the New Covenant lawyer's job is to point to the New Covenant, to declare, "You are released from shame; you are forgiven; you are free!" The job of the New Covenant lawyer (prophet) is to enforce God's New Covenant and its effects. This includes healing, deliverance, salvation, forgiveness, and a cleansed conscience.

No longer is the Spirit only on a few individuals, as in Old Covenant times, but now in the New Covenant the Spirit has been poured out to all. It is time for the whole Church to *"pursue the greater gifts..."* (1 Cor. 12:31), but *"especially prophecy"* (1 Cor. 14:1). This is our great honor!

Dr. Jonathan Welton
Bestselling Author & President of Welton Academy

Introduction

We were married in 1971. In 1972, we graduated from Bible school and entered directly into what eventually became known as the Discipleship/Shepherding Movement. Like many other young people, we were eager for more of God. We wanted to see miracles; we wanted to experience all God had for us. We longed to put into practice all we had learned during our years of study.

In those years directly following the Charismatic Renewal, college campuses across the country were dotted with student prayer and fellowship groups. We connected with one such group at a local university near our home. At least 95 percent of us in that group were under the age of twenty-five. The leadership consisted of three married couples—one in their thirties, one in their forties, and one in their sixties. None of these three lead couples knew much of the Bible. Thus began our journey.

The 1970s saw a real increase in prophecy and deliverance in the Church. It was exciting and new. However, even those who had been walking with the Lord for a long time in Pentecostal and charismatic circles didn't really know much about either subject. Not many leaders were teaching on these topics, and very little well-written scriptural material was available. As a result, people were polarized—one side afraid of the possible dangers of dabbling in prophecy or deliverance, the other side (including us) very interested in experiencing and learning. Unfortunately, neither side knew much about the benefits or dangers surrounding these subjects.

In the midst of this lack of understanding, those on the side eager to learn about and experience the prophetic jumped in head-first. It was a prophetic free-for-all, with no accountability or responsibility. People were free to function as they understood and as they saw fit. They could stop a person on the street or in the hall at church and give them "a word from the Lord." The trouble was, it was usually delivered as just that—"the Word of the Lord." It wasn't given or received with any understanding of the need to test prophetic words. Thus, those who received such "words" acted on them without testing, without counsel, and without prayer. We knew families who sold their homes, gave up jobs, and moved across the country or the world based solely on a "prophetic word" they received. Not knowing that testing prophecy is a scriptural principle, they put all their weight on one prophecy.

Many people were eager to know God and especially to hear from Him, and because of that, they were open to these so-called prophecies that were often controlling, manipulative, and heavy-handed. (I say *so-called* because, according to 1 Corinthians 14:3, prophecy is for the purpose of encouragement, comfort, and edification.). The so-called prophetic words gave very specific direction regarding people's lives, marriages, children, finances, and so forth. They delved into areas prophecy was never meant to go. In this unhealthy prophetic culture, we began to see our friends going into debt for appliances, furniture, and clothing they could not afford. People were told whether or not they should get married (and to whom), if and when they should have a baby, and when and where they should move. They were instructed on what clothing they should purchase, what jobs they should or should not take, and what offerings they should give to certain organizations. Couples who were struggling in their marriages were told through "prophetic words" to divorce, and as a result, families were broken up. People went into debt in order to buy brand new items in obedience to "prophecy." In reality, they would have been better off going to a garage sale and buying something within their budget. That would have been more honoring to the Lord than purchasing something they could

Introduction

not afford! Not surprisingly, many people were hurt and disappointed along the way. Many were led astray in the name of prophecy.

One friend of ours received a "prophetic word" about whom he should marry. However, the young lady mentioned in the "prophetic word" was not even walking with the Lord. This "word" followed him for a few years until he met another young lady whom he liked. In talking with her, he discovered they both loved the Lord and wanted to be missionaries. Into this scenario entered the problem of the "prophetic word." If that word was from the Holy Spirit, he reasoned, he should wait for God to fulfill it. What a dilemma—all because he had no teaching on the importance of testing a "word." He didn't know he could determine a "word" was not from the Holy Spirit at all. Thank God he received some wise counsel from a few older leaders! They were able to help him understand that prophecy is conditional and that sometimes it comes from someone's personal thoughts and desires (not the Holy Spirit). As a result, this particular young man realized discerning his life's direction involved more than one "prophetic word." He was able to determine a sound course for his life, married the second lady in the story, had a family, and spent several years on the mission field.

We were part of our campus group for seven and a half years. During that time, couples divorced and left the fellowship. Some, even to this day, do not walk with the Lord. They were hurt and disillusioned, and rather than attaching responsibility for all these problems to the people involved, too often they blamed the Lord. They questioned His Word and the gifts of the Holy Spirit (see 1 Cor. 12–14). Unfortunately, our group was not unusual; the same problems arose across the country. And over the course of ten or so years, people began to turn away from the use of these gifts. To a great degree, they disappeared from the scene.

Our personal journey continued another twenty years without much mention of or activity in prophecy, deliverance, or any of the other spiritual gifts. We believed in them, but we had no opportunity to learn about or use them. After what we had experienced, we were determined, if we were ever to get involved in this arena again, it must be rooted in a high level of integrity, accountability, and responsibility! We saw these gifts in the Scriptures, and we believed they were for our present day. With these two thoughts as our foundation, we began to search the Scriptures to let them speak for themselves. So began a whole new journey.

Much of what we learned about the prophetic is contained in this book, which started out as a thirty-page training manual for use in our local church. Now, in its expanded form, it is the accumulation of years of study, thought, and increased understanding. We trust you will find it enlightening and encouraging. Truly, God has given wonderful and helpful gifts to His Body for every generation to experience and be built upon.

one

In Defense of Prophecy

Years ago in a dream I saw a large package on the front corner of a church platform. This package was wrapped beautifully in a silver foil paper, tied with a professional-looking red bow, and displayed just so on a table. In the dream, I knew this gift had been on public display for a very long time. People would notice and comment on the beauty of this gift, and the leadership would say it was their gift, how beautiful it was, and how glad they were to have it. As they said this, I felt frustrated.

When I awoke, the Spirit shared His own frustration with me. He showed me that some churches have been given His gifts, but these gifts have never been opened or used. They are only acknowledged. They are displayed day-after-day, month-after-month, year-after-year, but no one quite knows how to open them or how to put them into use. It's simpler to leave them wrapped than to make all that mess by opening the package and then dealing with the immaturity that is part of the process of learning how to handle the gifts.

The problem with that approach is this: God us gave these gifts so we would use them to edify, comfort, encourage, protect, restore, provide for, and reveal His glory to His people, as well as to those who don't yet know Him. If we don't make the mess and take the time, we will miss out on so much that He meant us to have. His gifts were never meant to be like nice jewelry on a bracelet; they are tools He knew we would need in order to survive and thrive in our lives on earth. Donald Gee, author of *Concerning Spiritual Gifts*, offers a helpful perspective on this:

> It is easy to stand for these gifts in theory and in doctrine, but not to actually manifest them. A very big part of the purpose of God in the out-pouring of the Holy Spirit will be frustrated if we don't have the actual exercise or manifestation of these gifts functioning in our churches. One of the greatest reasons we don't allow the exercise of these gifts is the constant dread of error.[1]

For too many years, much of the Church has allowed fear or error to keep the spiritual gifts of God unopened and unused. Yet this, in itself, is deception. It is a purposeful alienation from God's purpose for our lives and His Church.

As we see in the Old Testament, a lack of the prophetic was always a sign something was wrong in the hearts of the people. For example, prior to the prophet Samuel's first encounter with God, as a young boy, the Bible tells us, *"In those days the word of the LORD was rare; there were not many visions"* (1 Sam. 3:1). In Psalm 74, Asaph cries out in anguish over the desperate and godless state of his nation, saying, *"We are given no signs from God; no prophets are left, and none of us knows how long this will be"* (Ps. 74:9). God explicitly states a lack of prophecy as a judgment against His sinful people:

> *...I will send a famine on the land—not a famine of food or a thirst for water, but a famine of hearing the words of the LORD. People will stagger from sea to sea and wander from north to east, searching for the word of the LORD, but they will not find it* (Amos 8:11–12).

In the New Covenant, God does not punish us with a lack of His word. Instead, He has poured out His Spirit on all and given His gifts to many. Therefore, the lack of prophecy in a church indicates a problem on our end, a fear or hardness or lack of receptivity toward God's gifts that has caused them to be quenched or overlooked. He is not holding back; we are. He has already released the prophetic gifts in our midst, so if we are not experiencing them, it is because we have chosen not to. Thus, the lack of prophecy shows us that something is wrong in our hearts, that we have embraced a form of deception regarding the gifts of the Spirit.

Because of this fear and deception, the gift of prophecy has taken a back seat in the Church and often been completely neglected. But it is an important part of the Christian life. As believers, we are not meant to live without it. For this reason, God is restoring this gift to the Church today, with more revelation about its purpose and usage. Fortunately, it is also being used with a greater measure of integrity and accountability than before. There has never been a better time to learn about and begin to experience the gift of prophecy.

And God wants us to do just that. He values prophecy because through it He communicates with people, both believers and unbelievers. He uses it to encourage us, stimulate us to action, comfort us, direct us, call forth the gifts in us, and confirm what He is speaking to us. He knew the Church would experience all sorts of trials and difficulties. In the midst of them, He knew we would need the full blessing inherent in the properly functioning gift of prophecy. We would need to hear His voice.

The New Testament confirms this. In First Corinthians 12–14 alone, we find six references to the edification of believers through the gift of prophecy. In his letter to the Corinthians, Paul placed such an emphasis on the importance of prophetic edification because he knew God desires a healthy and mature Church. One of the tools useful to such health and maturity is the gift of prophecy. The same is true of all nine manifestations (gifts) of the Holy Spirit; each is for building up, stimulating, and comforting the Church.

As we begin, let us be as the Bereans in Acts 17:11, who were *"of more noble character than those in Thessalonica, for they received the message with great eagerness and examined the Scriptures every day to see if what Paul said was true."* Everything presented in this book is subject to the test of the written Word of God—the Holy Bible. Thus, I encourage you to search these teachings out for yourself. Compare, pray, and consider all before the Lord; then decide for yourselves if the things taught here are good for equipping the people of God. A great difference exists between approaching new teaching with a humble, biblical search for truth and approaching it with the tendency to argue against and criticize. I encourage the first but not the second.

For many, the big question about prophecy is not just *why?* but *who?* Therefore, we must start our study of prophecy by examining Joel 2:28 and Acts 3:38–39 side-by-side:

> *Afterward, I will pour out my Spirit on **all** people. Your sons and daughters will prophesy, your old men will dream dreams, your young men will see visions* (Joel 2:28).

> *Peter replied…"The promise is for you and your children, and **for all who are far off**—for all whom the Lord our God will call"* (Acts 2:38–39).

On the day of Pentecost, the day recorded in Acts 2, the apostles did not prophesy, dream, or see visions. Yet the apostle Peter explained what was happening by pointing to Joel 2 and saying, *"This is that!"* Peter understood, by the Holy Spirit, that what was happening was, indeed, the beginning of the fulfillment of the promise in Joel 2:28–29. Joel's prophecy proclaimed once the Spirit was poured out, all people (not just a few, as in Old Covenant times) would receive prophetic words, dreams, and visions from God. The initial outpouring of the Spirit at Pentecost was meant to lead to these manifestations (and it did). It was only the beginning of the fulfillment of the New Covenant.

In Acts 2:39, which has been called the great equalizer, we find the answer to the question *who?* Clearly, this promise is meant for all, regardless of race, gender, age, or socio-economic class. It is all-inclusive. That means it includes us. Peter's reference to those *"who are far off"* has a dual application. First, it refers to the future. Anyone who would come into the realm of the Spirit after the day of Pentecost, no matter how many years later, would be included in this promise from Joel. Second, it refers to the Gentiles. Under the Old Covenant, the Gentiles were "far off" because they were not part of Israel and all of their covenant promises and blessings. As Paul wrote:

> *Remember that at that time you were separate from Christ, excluded from citizenship in Israel and foreigners to the covenants of the promise, without hope and without God in the world. But now in Christ Jesus you who once were far away have been brought near by the blood of Christ* (Ephesians 2:12–13).

Now all people are invited freely into covenant relationship with God, and that covenant includes the gift of prophecy. We all may prophesy.

In a day when New Age teachings and practices are rampant, many Christians fear or shy away from the use of the biblical spiritual gifts, considering them dangerous. What we must remember is that they are *our* gifts. They belong to the Church, and the enemy is simply counterfeiting them to deceive people and keep them in darkness. He is also in the business of stealing what belongs to us. John 10:10 says, *"The thief comes only to steal and to kill and to destroy...."* He is able to do this when we are not convinced the gifts *do* belong to us.

God, on the other hand, wants us to know what belongs to us and how to use these gifts for the benefit of others. In First Corinthians 12:1, Paul says he does not want the body to be unaware, ignorant, or uninformed regarding the spiritual gifts. The way to avoid ignorance is to be taught. Thus, God wants us to learn how to use the gifts properly, how to discern when they are being used improperly, and how to use them to bless others in the love of God. The answer to the potential dangers is not to stay as far away from the gifts as possible so we don't become deceived. In fact, when we remain ignorant and fearful of the gifts of the Holy Spirit, we are living in deception already. The enemy has deceived us into believing the gifts are not for today or they are only for certain people to use. He even claims we cannot be taught and trained in how to use them in our own lives. If we listen to his lies and choose to fear these manifestations of the Spirit, the thief has already stolen from us. Our fear will keep them from us.

God has something much better for us. He has given us good gifts, and He wants us to know how to use them so we can hear Him speak and be encouraged. When we look to Scripture, we see God intends the prophetic as a magnificent blessing to His Church. He has a grand and glorious purpose for prophecy. If we will open up the gift He has given us, it will change our lives.

God's Word: An Anchor

The first step in a healthy understanding of the biblical gift of prophecy is knowing the standard it must be measured by—which is always and only the Word of God. We believe the Bible alone contains the written Word of God. It is the final authority on every subject. Because it has been transcribed and translated so many times throughout the centuries, we must study it seriously in a historical, contextual exegesis in order to best understand God's original meaning.

By *Scriptures* we mean both the Old Testament and the New Testament, commonly known as the Holy Bible. We believe the Bible is the final authority by which we may judge all things. That means, if our opinions differ from the Bible, we are the ones who must change. We must make the adjustments. We must never dismiss or disregard it just because it may be contrary to something we believe. When we come to the Bible, we must always approach it with an open mind and a teachable heart in order to receive what the Holy Spirit desires to reveal to us. This principle is found in Romans 3:4, which says, *"Let God be true, and every human being a liar…."* Here we see the belief that no matter what arises that might seem to bring God and His ways into question, He is always right and true. If someone is wrong or lying, it is not God. He cannot lie, and neither does His Word. Instead, as Paul wrote:

> *The word of God is alive and active. Sharper than any double-edged sword, it penetrates even to dividing soul and spirit, joints and marrow; it judges the thoughts and attitudes of the heart* (Hebrews 4:12).

This is orthodox Christian belief about the Bible. A common fear about prophecy is that it seeks to add to the Scriptures. This is absolutely not true. Whenever material is added to the Scripture, a cult is formed. That is not the purpose of prophecy. Rather, prophecy in the body of Christ simply means hearing a message from the Lord and delivering it to a person or group of people. Because the Bible is our standard for truth, everything said in a prophetic message should be tested against it. If anything does not align with the sound doctrine of the Scriptures, it is to be discarded. Prophecy is not above, beyond, nor outside of the Scriptures. Instead, it is subject to the Scriptures. In other words, it must be examined very carefully to determine whether it aligns with the truth of the written Word and with the nature of God as revealed in the Bible.

This is why it is so important to obey the apostle Paul's command to test all things: *"Do not treat prophecies with contempt but test them all; hold on to what is good"* (1 Thess. 5:20–21). When Paul says to hold on to what is good, he implies some of it may not be good. And that we should let go of. We will discuss the testing process in more depth in a later chapter, but for now, the important point is that we must test all prophecies against the ultimate truth of the Bible.

We also see the importance of the standard of the gospel in Galatians 1:6–9:

> *I am astonished that you are so quickly deserting the one who called you to live in the grace of Christ and are turning to a different gospel—which is really no gospel at all. Evidently some people are throwing you into confusion and are trying to pervert the gospel of Christ. But even if we or an angel from heaven should preach a gospel other than the one we*

> *preached to you, let them be under God's curse. As we have already said, so now I say again: If anybody is preaching to you a gospel other than what you accepted, let them be under God's curse.*

In Paul's day, some Christians were allowing themselves to be deceived by teachings that contradicted the gospel message, and he strongly warned them to ignore any word or experience that contradicted the truth found in Christ. The same is true for us today. We cannot allow ourselves to be deceived by an experience, a person, or an angel that contradicts the Word of God. Even if an angel would come to us and speak to us about something outside of the gospel of Christ, as written in the Scriptures, we must not receive or believe the angel. Instead, we must consider the angel cursed. Joseph Smith believed the unbiblical teachings of an "angel" (really a demon masquerading as an angel) who appeared to him, and as a result, he formed the cult we know as Mormonism. We do not want to follow in his footsteps.

The point is this: We cannot base our faith and doctrine on experiences alone. We must base them on the Word of God and the character of God as revealed in the Word. We cannot allow ourselves to be mesmerized by the idea that an angel or someone we admire is teaching us. If it is against the clear doctrines of God in the Scriptures, it doesn't matter who is saying it. It is wrong. No new revelation exists outside or beyond the written Scriptures. New revelation is only found within the Scriptures. The Holy Spirit continually enlightens our minds to understand more of what is written within the pages of the Bible. In this way, we grow in understanding, both individually and corporately. But nothing extra may be added alongside the Bible or counted as equal to it. Nothing. As soon as we allow that to happen, we have the beginnings of a cult.

The Bible is so important because it is an anchor for us, helping us to hold fast to the truth in the midst of life's sometimes tumultuous or confusing experiences. Experiences are subjective; only the written Word of God is objective. Only it can be our foundation. That doesn't mean it's wrong to have experiences and revelation; what it means is that our experiences and revelation must always be tested for validity against the Scriptures. When we have the Scriptures as our anchor, we can freely enter into the sea of experiences without fear. Even when goofy things happen or people wander away from the faith or the Spirit moves in ways we have never experienced before, we know we have the Word as our anchor, and it never changes. It is the safe place—the constant—in the spiritual life.

What we base our faith on really matters. If the Scriptures are not our objective anchor, holding us secure in this ocean of life, we can be carried away downstream, and we may even drown. What we believe is very important to our lives in God. Doctrine matters. I have heard many people minimize the importance of doctrine, saying they are not into "all that doctrine stuff" because it's too hard for them to understand.

However, the definition of *doctrine* is simply "teaching and instruction." Understanding doctrine doesn't mean we need a degree in theology. It does mean we need to understand and walk in the basic and foundational teachings of the Scripture well enough that we are able to teach others. The writer of Hebrews makes this priority clear:

> *In fact, though by this time you ought to be teachers, you need someone to teach you the elementary truths of God's word all over again. You need milk, not solid food! Anyone who lives on milk, being still an infant, is not acquainted with the teaching about righteousness. But solid food is for the mature, who by constant use have trained themselves to distinguish good from evil* (Hebrews 5:12–14).

The very first believers diligently devoted themselves to learning the doctrine of the faith: *"They devoted themselves to the apostles' teaching [doctrine] and to fellowship, to the breaking of bread and to prayer"* (Acts 2:42). They gathered daily to, among other things, be continually taught the apostles' doctrine. Many of these believers were simple, everyday people who were not highly educated or even highly intelligent. But they knew the need to understand, and they were eager to learn what this faith in Christ was all about. The same must be true for believers today, both new believers and those who have been in the faith for a long time. We never outgrow our need to learn and to come to fuller understanding (and experience) of the basics of the gospel. And when we allow the Spirit to continue to lead us into all truth, He will build in us an understanding of the Scriptures and doctrine that will truly serve as an anchor during the difficulties of life.

As Paul writes, the Scripture keeps us close to the truth:

> *All Scripture is God-breathed and is useful for teaching, rebuking, correcting, and training in righteousness so that the servant of God may be thoroughly equipped for every good work* (2 Timothy 3:16–17).

Of course, the fact that the Scripture is our anchor does not mean interpreting it is as simple as picking out one verse that seems to support what we want it to. Responsible study of the Word of God involves considering the whole counsel of the Word, both Old and New Testaments. It means accounting for the revealed nature of God and His dealings with humans. As the writer of Hebrews warned, *"Jesus Christ is the same yesterday and today and forever. Do not be carried away by all kinds of strange teachings. It is good for our hearts to be strengthened by grace…"* (Heb. 13:8–9). God's character, as revealed in the Bible, does not change. Any genuine new revelation will align with His character and the teaching of Scripture. This means we cannot pick-and-choose as we like, finding verses that (out of context) seem to back up what we want to believe He is saying to us.

When counteracting false teachings in the early Church, Paul wrote to the early believers, exhorting them to hold on to the gospel truth that Paul had written to them:

> *If anyone thinks they are a prophet or otherwise gifted by the Spirit, let them acknowledge that what I am writing to you is the Lord's command. But if anyone ignores this, they will themselves be ignored* (1 Corinthian 14:37–38).

This gospel truth is the written Word of God. We must never take a verse out of context or interpret it in a way that contradicts the rest of the Word. Being faithful stewards of the written Word of God is very important (see 1 Tim. 4:16; 2 Tim. 2:15).

For this reason, we must approach the written Word as students, with humility, allowing it to teach us. We must subject ourselves to its scrutiny, not make it come under our scrutiny. Whenever we come to the Scriptures, we must pray, read, and compare one section with another, always reading the words in context and always allowing the words to speak for themselves, without superimposing our opinions over top of them. When we do this, the outcome may be completely different from what we have been taught previously. (See 2 Peter 1:16–21.)

Too often doctrines are passed from generation to generation by way of tradition, without thorough study and reexamination of the Scripture. Certain denominations believe certain things, and for them, that's final! Those doctrines are never open to reinterpretation. However, the truth is, no denomination's teachings are final; only the written Word is final. Denominations have come into being throughout history because of new truths being discovered in the Scriptures. It is sad when groups formed around a willingness to consider revising their understanding of Scripture evolve into a rigidity that does not allow for any further revelation.

Instead, our attitude must be the same as David's, as expressed in Psalm 119, a Psalm of adoration for God's Word:

In what way can a person keep his life pure? By guarding it according to your word. Your word have I hidden in my heart so that I won't sin against you (Psalm 119:9–11).

When we value the Word like that, as an anchor of truth for our lives and for all spiritual experiences and revelations, we will be safe from deception and empowered to dive deeper into the fullness of God's truth, including the spiritual gifts He gives us. A solid foundation in His Word is the prerequisite for godly, healthy use of the gift of prophecy.

three

Restoration: The Framework

The second piece essential to a healthy understanding of the biblical gift of prophecy is a revelation of God's heart of restoration. It is the core of the gospel message, and if we don't get it, we will not be able to accurately convey God's heart through prophecy.

According to *Webster's New Universal Unabridged Dictionary*, the word *restoration* carries with it many meanings, including:

1. to give back or bring back; to return to a person, as a specific thing which he has lost or which has been taken from him and unjustly detained. to make restitution of; as, to restore lost or stolen goods to the owner

2. to put a person back into a former position, place, rank, or condition; to replace, to return to a former place

3. to bring back to a former or normal condition, as by repairing, rebuilding, altering, etc, as to restore a building or a painting

4. to bring back to health, strength, etc

5. to re-establish something which has passed away, as a custom, a system of government, etc.

Synonyms of *restoration* include: repay, return, replace, renew, refund, repair, recover, and heal. Contained in this definition is the heart of God for all people. This is His bottom line for planet earth. It's why He sent Jesus, and it's why He empowers us as His ambassadors. If we want to partner with Him in the expanding of His Kingdom on earth, we need to carry this same vision. Restoration must be our heartbeat. It must be the mindset—the framework—that informs everything else we do.

Whether or not we truly believe God's desire is *always* for redemption, restoration, reconciliation, deliverance, freedom, and liberty will make all the difference in our attempts to hear from God for ourselves or others. It will influence *what* we hear and *how* we present what we have heard to others. When the Holy Spirit speaks something to us about someone else, we are responsible to steward that word properly. When He whispers, we must ask Him how we should present the information He has given us. This is where restoration comes into the picture. If we understand the Holy Spirit's desire to bring life—not death and judgment—it will make all the difference in how we present prophetic words.

Suppose a young lady comes to you for prayer and the Holy Spirit shows you she was the victim of sexual abuse as a young child and again as a young teenager. Now she lives a life of drugs and prostitution. That is precious information, entrusted into your hands by the Holy Spirit. He is trusting you to handle it restoratively. The outcome in this young lady's life will depend on how you present this information. If you handle it immaturely and judgmentally by simply passing along the facts, she might seem fine outwardly, but chances are she will feel so embarrassed and exposed that she will leave you (and church) and may never return again. This is a misuse of the word of knowledge and prophecy, because she did not leave encouraged or stimulated to take action to change her life. First Corinthians 14:3 says, *"But the one who prophesies speaks to people for their strengthening, encouraging and comfort"* (1 Cor. 14:3). It is not enough to just share the information we receive from the Holy Spirit; we must work hand-in-hand with Him to bring about restorative change in people's lives.

Here's another option, a more redemptive and restorative way to share the information you received from the Holy Spirit. You could say something like, "The Holy Spirit has shown me that when you were a little child you were mistreated and had some traumatic experiences, which happened again when you were a bit older." By this point, the young lady will probably have tears in her eyes or running down her face. She knows what you're talking about, but you have not completely exposed her to anyone else who might be listening or ministering with you. Then you could continue, "He loves you so much, and it grieves Him deeply that you were a victim to these experiences. Because of those experiences, you have made some poor choices for your life, some of which you are involved in right now. But He wants to come close to you, save your life, and set you free to walk with Him. He has a wonderful plan for your life if you are willing to give yourself to Him today." Then, depending on her response, you can continue to share and speak of His love and plans, bringing her to salvation knowledge of Jesus Christ and the freedom that He died to give her.

How we steward the information the Holy Spirit whispers to us is very, very important. The results are a matter of life or death in people. We must be faithful representatives of His heart of restoration toward people.

When our children were growing up and still lived at home, we could leave one of the older ones in charge while we went out for a while. Often we would ask that older child to pass along a message to the others for us. We might say something like, "We'll be back in a couple hours. While we're gone, please tell the others we want them to do their homework and finish their chores. Then, when we return, we can all have pizza and watch a movie or play some games." That was our heart as parents, to be able to spend time with our kids and enjoy time together as a family. However, the heart behind the message could have very easily been distorted if it was passed along like this: "Dad said you guys need to do your homework and finish your chores, or when he gets back, you're going to be in so much trouble!" Do you hear the difference? The facts are there, but the heart and character of the parents is missing. Sadly, this is too often the way our heavenly

Father's children present His messages to others. They pass along the truth accurately, but not the heart. And without the heart, the message is distorted. Unfortunately, people who prophesy like this often have never experienced the heart of their heavenly Father either. They may have been Christians for many years, but they have a distorted view of God; they see Him as a harsh, angry, and judgmental Father. They have completely misunderstood His heart. He is not harsh, angry, or judgmental, but unfortunately, many believers are taught to see Him like that. This is why knowing His heart is so important to prophetic ministry. We cannot accurately deliver His messages of restoration if we believe He is angry and judgmental.

We have discovered, no matter where we are in the world, when we teach on prophecy, the first question people asked is, "What about judgment?" See, in the Old Testament, God's prophets often delivered harsh and judgmental words against individuals and nations. Back then, He often seemed angry and frightening. This question about judgment is important if we want to consider the whole counsel of the Word of God. In my desire to answer this question biblically, I decided to read through the Old Testament prophets, both major and minor. I ended up reading through them several times, searching for God's heart in these writings. *What was He really saying, and why? How does this Old Testament picture fit with the New Testament picture of Jesus?* The conclusion I finally came to is this: The God of the Old Testament is, indeed, the same as the God in the New Testament. He is a loving, caring God whose main desire is for His people to have close relationship with Him so He can bless them.

Too often we believe the New Testament God is different from the Old Testament God. We think the God of the Old Testament was judgmental and harsh, speaking only woes and punishments. This, however, is an inaccurate perception. Within the writings of the Old Testament prophets we find God's heart of tenderness and His longing for His people to walk with Him so He could bless them. When they went astray, He yearned for them to return to Him. When they rebelled and hardened their hearts against Him, He sent His prophets to plead with them to return to Him and repent. We hear this heart cry when

He laments through Hosea, *"How can I give you up, O Ephraim? How can I hand you over, O Israel?...My heart is turned over within Me, all My compassions are kindled"* (Hos. 11:8 NASB). And in Amos the pain of the betrayal rings over and over in His simple statement, *"Yet you have not returned to me"* (Amos 4:6, 8, 9, 10, 11).

God went to great extents in an attempt to turn His people back to Him, because He loved and wanted them, but they were unwilling:

> *This is what the sovereign LORD, the Holy One of Israel, says: "In repentance and rest is your salvation, in quietness and trust is your strength, but you would have none of it"* (Isaiah 30:15).

Isaiah 44 gives us insight into the reality of what God was facing in His children. Deliberately and persistently, they had turned away from Him and set their hearts to idolatry. Because of this, He said, *"They know nothing, they understand nothing"* (verse 18), and, *"No one stops to think, no one has the knowledge or understanding"* (verse 19). They could not recognize the illogical and futile nature of idol worship. Instead, *"Such a person feeds on ashes; a deluded heart misleads him; he cannot save himself, or say, "Is not this thing in my right hand a lie?"* (verse 20).

The people were no longer able to think sensibly. Their hearts and minds had been dulled to depravity through rejecting God and choosing idols instead. Still, in the midst of this, God's heart for redemption and restoration shines through:

> *Remember these things, Jacob, for you, Israel, are my servant. I have made you, you are my servant; I will not forget you. I have swept your offenses like a cloud, your sins like the morning mist.* **Return to me**, *for I have redeemed you* (Isaiah 44:21–22).

In these verses, God was calling His idolatrous people to repentance. He was pleading with them to remember who they were and who He is and to choose to return to Him. Through Jeremiah, He called, *"Return, faithless people; I will cure you of backsliding"* (Jer. 3:22). The Knox translation renders this verse: *"Wandering hearts, come back to me, and all your rebel acts shall be pardoned"* (Jer. 3:22 Knox). God promised to remove the judgment their actions deserved and to restore them to relationship with Him if only they would return:

> *Do not be afraid, Jacob, my servant; do not be dismayed, Israel. I will surely save you out of a distant place, your descendants from their land of exile. Jacob will again have peace and security, and no one will make him afraid* (Jeremiah 46:27).

When His people did not repent and return to Him, God had to allow the consequences of their sinful choices to overtake them. We see this principle modeled in Daniel 4, which contains the Babylonian king Nebuchadnezzar's dream and the interpretation Daniel gave him. After explaining the meaning of the dream, Daniel advised the king:

> *Therefore, Your Majesty, be pleased to accept my advice: Renounce your sins by doing what is right, and your wickedness by being kind to the oppressed. It may be that then your prosperity will continue* (Daniel 4:27).

We see, from the next verse, that the king did not take Daniel's advice: *"All this happened to King Nebuchadnezzar"* (Dan. 4:28). Even though God wanted Nebuchadnezzar to repent and live rightly before Him, Nebuchadnezzar refused. He continued on in pride, as is evident in his statement, twelve months after God's warning, *"Is not this the great Babylon I have built as the royal residence, by my mighty power and for the glory of my majesty?"* (Dan. 4:30). God had given Nebuchadnezzar an entire year to repent, but his heart had not changed. Therefore, judgment came upon him because of his own choice (not God's) and his refusal to listen to God's pleading.

None of the punishments were new ideas God devised against His people. They were the natural outflow of the consequences put forth in Deuteronomy 28. Disobedience carries with it built-in consequences (curses), just like obedience carries with it built-in consequences (blessings). The problem wasn't on His end but on the end of His unfaithful people. His heart longed for restoration.

In all this, we can see how much God loves people. His desire is for the restoration of their lives so they can live in all the blessings He has provided for them. He is not sitting in Heaven as an angry judge with clenched fists. He is, instead, a loving heavenly Father who longs to be close to His children and bless them. His stance toward those who do not yet know Him is not anger or judgment but love and longing. He longs to welcome them home as His children. He longs to save them from destruction and welcome them into eternal life with Him.

This is exactly why He sent Jesus into the world to create a way for weak and sinful humanity to have close relationship with Him. This is what the Bible means when it says:

> *God, after He spoke long ago to the fathers in the prophets in many portions and in many ways, in these last days has spoken to us in His Son, whom He appointed heir of all things, through whom also He made the world. And He is the radiance of His glory* **and the exact representation of His nature**, *and upholds all things by the word of His power...* (Hebrews 1:1–3 NASB).

Jesus did not come into the world as a new God or an arbitrator between us and an angry Father. No—He came as the exact representation of Father God's nature and character. He came to show us what God's heart is really like. He came to show us that *"God so loved the world that he gave his one and only Son, that whoever believes in him shall not perish but have eternal life"* (John 3:16). As Paul says, that kind of love is uncommon and unfathomable:

> *Very rarely will anyone die for a righteous person, though for a good person someone might possibly dare to die. But God demonstrates his own love for us in this: While we were still sinners, Christ died for us* (Romans 5:7–8)

The fact that God sent His own Son to die for us, before we had repented, shows the depths of His heart of love and restoration toward us. This is the core of the gospel message, and it must be the frame of every prophecy we deliver.

four

The Prophetic Pyramid

Now that we've established the importance of the written Word of God as an anchor and God's heart of restoration as a framework, let's examine the biblical gift of prophecy and the various ways in which it manifests. The way prophecy works in the Church, or the difference between different types of prophetic gifts, is simply illustrated by this diagram of a pyramid:

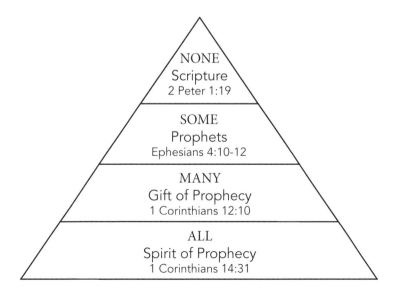

This diagram will clarify the various biblical terms related to prophecy that have, too often, caused confusion. This happens when several people talk about prophecy while each having a different understanding of what the terms being used mean. To avoid such confusion, in this chapter we will explain, as clearly as possible, the definitions behind the terms we use throughout this book. As we do this, we will also answer these common questions about prophecy:

1. Is everyone who prophesies a prophet?
2. Are New Testament and the Old Testament prophecy the same?
3. Is the supernatural gift of prophecy meant for only a select number of very spiritual people?
4. Does a word of prophecy carry the same weight as the written Word of God?

Let's start with the bottom line of the triangle, which illustrates the first point: All may prophesy through the Spirit of prophecy.

All - The Spirit of Prophecy

Under the New Covenant, all believers can prophesy through the spirit of prophecy, which has been poured out on all. We see this in First Corinthians 14:31, which says, *"For **you can all** prophesy in turn so that everyone may be instructed and encouraged."*

We know if something was mentioned or experienced in the Old Covenant, we can expect the New Covenant to include at least that much, and so much more, since the New is unfathomably better! Of course the least would be included in the greater. As Hebrews tells us, *"...Jesus has become the guarantor of a better covenant"* (Heb. 7:22), and, *"The ministry Jesus has received is as superior to theirs as the covenant of which he is mediator is superior to the old one, since the new covenant is established on better promises"* (Heb. 8:6). This includes prophecy.

In the Old Covenant, the Holy Spirit would come upon a particular person, chosen by God as His prophet or His voice to His people. If people wanted to hear from God or know His purpose, they would take a bag of coins and go on a journey to meet with the man of God. Usually one or two of them existed at any particular time as a prophet to either Judah or Israel. Now, under the New Covenant, all who have entered into relationship with God through the blood of Jesus Christ have received the Holy Spirit. The Spirit of God resides in us at all times; He does not come and go like He did during the Old Covenant days.

If we have received God's gift of salvation and have been filled with His Spirit, we now have the ability to hear from Him directly. Thus, the purpose of the gift of prophecy has changed. We don't need to look to the select "man of God" to hear God's voice. We can all hear Him. Instead, God has given prophecy to us so we may partner with Him in bringing encouragement and comfort and stimulating one another to continue walking in obedience with Him. We have the privilege of hearing personally and directly from Him through other believers, as well as delivering His words to others.

The Spirit of Prophecy in the Old Covenant

To fully understand this privilege, we need to first look back to the shadows of this New Covenant reality in the Old Covenant. For example, when Joshua was offended that certain elders in Israel began to prophesy by the Spirit, Moses rebuked him, saying *"Are you zealous for my sake? I wish that all the LORD's people were prophets and that the LORD would put his Spirit on them"* (Num. 11:29). What the elders experienced in this story was a temporary impartation. After Moses imparted the Spirit from himself to them, they prophesied. But it only happened that one time. *"When the Spirit rested on them, they prophesied—but did not do so again"* (Num. 11:25). The Spirit came on them and spoke through them, but only in that one setting.

Moses, as a prophet of God, knew how good it was to hear from God; consequently, he wished all God's people were prophets, that the Lord would put His Spirit on all of them. In that desire, he grasped, to some degree, what an encouraging and uplifting situation it would be if everyone were to hear from and speak for God! He saw a shadow of the New Covenant reality.

Joshua, however, did not understand. He was taken up with "the way things should be." He was watching out for Moses and trying to do everything the way Moses said it should be done. Joshua was especially disturbed by the fact that two of the elders who were not at the Tabernacle—where they were supposed to be—still began prophesying right where they were. This violated his understanding of what was right and orderly. This is why Moses asked him, *"Are you zealous for my sake?"* Joshua may have been trying to protect Moses' role as leader. But Moses realized it was not about him, but about God.

When Joshua brought this "disturbance of the peace" to Moses' attention, he expected Moses to correct the two elders. Instead, he spoke out what was in his heart; we might say he prophesied, because he spoke what was also in God's heart—the desire that everyone would be able to know His mind and share it with others for encouragement, comfort, and stimulation to action.

We find another Old Testament example of the Spirit of God coming upon someone, causing him to prophesy even though he was not one of the prophets of God, in the story of Saul. In the process of Saul being chosen as Israel's first king, God's prophet Samuel prophesied to Saul:

> *...As you approach the town, you will meet a procession of prophets coming down from the high place with lyres, timbrels, pipes and harps being played before them, and they will be prophesying. The Spirit of the LORD will come powerfully upon you, and you will prophesy with them; and you will be changed into a different person* (1 Samuel 10:5–6).

All this happened exactly as Samuel said it would, and Saul prophesied when the Spirit of God came upon him and gave him a new heart.

> *As Saul turned to leave Samuel, God changed Saul's heart, and all these signs were fulfilled that day. When he and his servant arrived at Gibeah, a procession of prophets met him;* ***the Spirit of God came powerfully upon him, and he joined in their prophesying.*** *When all those who had formerly known him saw him prophesying with the prophets, they asked each other, "What is this that has happened to the son of Kish? Is Saul also among the prophets?"* (1 Samuel 10: 9–11).

When Saul was with the group of prophets, he could prophesy and he did so. When he left them, he ceased to prophesy. The Bible only records one other time when Saul prophesied, and again, it was in the presence of prophets, when the Spirit of God came upon him (see 1 Sam. 19:18–24).

In these stories from the lives of Moses and Saul, we see that at specific times and places certain individuals temporarily received the ability to prophesy, even though in their everyday lives they did not prophesy. Seemingly, an anointing or atmosphere for prophecy rested on Moses and on the group of prophets—a shadow of what was to come under the New Covenant, when *all* would be able to prophesy.

The Spirit of Prophecy in the New Covenant

According to Ephesians 4:11–13, prophets also exist in the New Covenant Church. We will discuss New Covenant prophets in more detail at another level of the prophecy pyramid. But for our purposes here, it is important to note that when believers are in the presence of a mature prophet, learning from him or her, they come under the prophet's "umbrella" of anointing. A prophetic atmosphere is available, and they may enter into it. If they do, they may begin to prophesy or have dreams and visions, even if they have never done so before.

And those who have prophesied, dreamed, and had visions before will experience increase in these areas.

But unlike Saul and the elders who experienced this in Old Covenant times, believers today can continue to operate in the prophetic even after the prophet leaves the building. Certainly, some realities may interfere with individuals' ability to continue in the impartation they received from the prophet, but the possibility is there. They may need more teaching to understand how the gifts operate. They may need opportunities to practice. They may also need to find a group of people who understand the gifts so they can learn in community. All these pieces are important and helpful, but the bottom line is that believers can continue to prophesy through the Spirit of prophecy, even when no prophet is around.

In fact, in the New Covenant, we don't even need to have a prophet with us, because we can all prophesy. When we get together with a group of likeminded people, set aside time to be quiet before the Lord to listen to what He is saying, and acknowledge the Holy Spirit's presence, we will feel His presence and begin to hear Him speak. If the gathering is a practice session for the prophetic, we can take turns listening and sharing what we believe God is speaking to us. In this sort of environment we can experience the Spirit of prophecy, which is an atmosphere in which all can tune into Him and understand what is on His heart.

The apostle Paul talked about this sort of thing in his first letter to the Corinthian church. He said:

> *Two or three prophets should speak, and the others should weigh carefully what is said. And if a revelation comes to someone who is sitting down, the first speaker should stop. For you can all prophesy in turn so that everyone may be instructed and encouraged. The spirits of prophets are subject to the control of prophets. For God is not a God of disorder but of peace—as in all the congregations of the Lord's people* (1 Corinthians 14:29–33).

Here he gives instructions for how to keep the meeting orderly and focused. Paul mentions having *"two or three"* speak because *"two or three"* was a principle throughout the Jewish community. Whenever the idea of witnesses was brought up, it was always at the mouth of *"two or three."* This was first established in Deuteronomy 17. Paul was not setting up a regulation regarding prophecy or saying if a fourth person prophesied it would be out of order. He was simply addressing the idea that in the mouth of *"two or three"* the heart of the Lord would be revealed and confirmed in that particular meeting. Therefore, if you have a practice session and open it for everyone to share what they are receiving, you are not out of order biblically. It is not about an exact number but about putting some parameters around the prophetic in a congregational meeting and thereby creating a measure of order.

Once the spirit of prophecy begins flowing, anyone who plugs in can know what the Spirit is saying. And in an open meeting, any or all can enter in and flow in prophecy. This is another reason why Paul put the borders of *"two or three"* around this area. He understood that once *"two or three"* had spoken out, the main thoughts had been revealed, and that was enough—for the sake of time in a congregational meeting.

In this we see the reality that the shadow of the Spirit of prophecy revealed in the Old Covenant has been fleshed out in a much greater experience for us in the New Covenant. No longer is it an occasional and unexpected event when a person is filled with the Spirit and begins to prophesy. No longer does the ability to prophesy come and go. Now we all can walk in the Spirit of prophecy at any time. Now the prophetic anointing flows frequently and richly when believers gather to listen to His voice.

Now, let's look at the second level of the prophetic pyramid—the gift of prophecy given to some believers.

Some—The Gift of Prophecy

Moving up the pyramid, we see that the space designated for the gift of prophecy is not as broad as that for the Spirit of prophecy. This illustrates the fact that the gift is not all-inclusive in the way the Spirit is. Not everyone has the gift of prophecy. But a lot more people have this gift than many of us realize. The biblical foundation for the gift of prophecy is found in Romans 12:4–8. As part of a longer list of spiritual gifts, Paul writes, *"We have different gifts, according to the grace given to each of us. If your gift is prophesying, then prophesy in accordance with your faith"* (Rom. 12:6).

In First Corinthians 12:8–10, Paul gives us another list of nine different gifts given by the Holy Spirit to the body of Christ. All of these gifts spring forth from the realm of the Spirit. They do not come from our natural minds, talents, or abilities. One of these gifts is the gift of prophecy: *"...to another* [is given the gift of] *prophecy..."* (1 Cor. 12:10).

Desiring the Gift of Prophecy

Some people have the gift of prophecy and do not realize it because they have never been taught about it or they go to churches that teach the gifts of the Spirit ceased after the first century. Others may not have the gift of prophecy, but they desire to have it. In this case, individuals who want the gift of prophecy can ask a leader who has the gift of prophecy to lay hands on them and impart the gift to them. We see this possibility in Paul's words to the Romans, *"I long to see you so that I may impart to you some spiritual gift to make you strong"* (Rom. 1:11), as well as his exhortation to the Corinthians, *"Follow the way of love and eagerly desire* [covet] *gifts of the Spirit, especially prophecy"* (1 Cor. 14:1). Through Paul's injunction to desire or covet the gift of prophecy, we see that people who want it can ask for it and believe they will receive it. The word *covet* means "to be zealous for something, to burn with desire, to pursue ardently, to desire eagerly or intensely."[2] Our Father would not have encouraged us to covet or desire something so strongly if He did not intend to give it to us.

If you desire the gift of prophecy, simply ask God for it. He has not reserved it for only a few. Some teachers use First Corinthians 12:11 to suggest the Holy Spirit distributes the gifts as He chooses; the way they see it, if you have the gift of prophecy, you have it, and if you don't, you don't. People who think this way will say things like, "I'm just not prophetic." They state it as a settled fact. But this is not how the Bible presents the spiritual gifts. It is poor scholarship to take one verse and build a belief around it alone. We must compare verse with verse and also study verses within context. In this context, that means comparing the verse that says God distributes the gifts as He wills alongside the verse that tells us to earnestly desire the gift of prophecy.

As parents, if our children desired something so much that they were always reading about it, looking at pictures of it, praying about it, talking about it, saving up their own money to have it, and talking to other people who already have it, we would want to give it to them. This would be even more the case if what they greatly desired was something that would be extremely beneficial to them and others. This is what it means to earnestly desire (covet) the best gifts, especially prophecy. Any good parent would be moved by that kind of a heart. And God is the best parent, as Jesus pointed out when He said:

> *...Ask and it will be given to you; seek and you will find; knock and the door will be opened to you. For everyone who asks receives; the one who seeks finds; and to the one who knocks, the door will be opened. Which of you fathers, if your son asks for a fish, will give him a snake instead? Or if he asks for an egg, will give him a scorpion? If you then, though you are evil, know how to give good gifts to your children, how much more will your Father in heaven give the Holy Spirit to those who ask him* (Luke 11:9–13).

Among all the spiritual gifts, we are especially exhorted to covet the gift of prophecy. Why is this gift singled out as special? I believe it is because Paul understood how very important the gift of prophecy is to the body of Christ. He knew it would encourage and strengthen people when they were weak and afraid; it would comfort them when they were stricken with grief and loneliness or faced persecution; it would stir them up to step out and act in faith. As mentioned previously, at six places in First Corinthians 12 and 14 the gift of prophecy is referred to as a source of edification or strengthening for the body of Christ. The Holy Spirit knew the troubles believers would face and the encouragement they would need, and as a result, He decided to give prophecy as one of the nine gifts of the Spirit.

Prophecy is also the channel through which the other eight gifts mentioned can function freely. The word *prophecy* can be explained several ways. It means "to speak forth or flow forth." It can bubble up like an artesian well. It can mean "to announce something or to speak for God." It is divinely inspired speech. It may be a declaration. When we as God's people learn to quiet our souls and tune our spirits to what the Holy Spirit wants to say to us and others around us, we can become vessels through whom God can speak His prophetic words. We tune into the spiritual realm, become aware of God's heart and mind for a particular person or body of believers, and yield our minds and tongues to His use—thus enabling Him to share His thoughts with others.

Stewarding the Gift of Prophecy

Some who have the gift of prophecy may not know it. In them the gift is dormant. Others have had the opportunity to learn, practice, and step out in faith in this area often. This training and practice enables them to advance and become quite proficient at hearing the voice of the Lord and sharing it with others. With the gift of prophecy, a great deal depends upon how a person stewards the gift. Having a spiritual gift does not make certain people any more spiritual than others. It does call them to step forward, be obedient, and learn how to steward their gift. Walking in the gifts of the Spirit is a great responsibility, and it should be taken seriously. We have visited churches where the gifts of prophecy and healing were treated as charms on a bracelet, as something extra to add to the plethora of other activities available. This is not how God wants us to view His gifts to us. He wants us to cherish and honor them as we would priceless gifts from a king—because that is what they are.

Part of stewarding the spiritual gifts is knowing what gifts God has given us. If you don't know, ask Him. And ask Him, particularly, if He has given you the gift of prophecy. If you seem to know things before they happen, if you frequently have dreams or thoughts that then come to pass, you probably have the gift of prophecy. People who have the gift of prophecy also tend to have a real interest in supernatural things, things outside this natural realm. If you have an awareness that more exists than what you experience with your five senses, you probably have the gift of prophecy. Unfortunately, many people, even Christians, do not understand biblical prophecy. Some are afraid of it or opposed to it. Regardless of what they think, you can be assured that the gift of prophecy is a gift from God, and He wants you to use it and grow in it. If others don't understand or even persecute you for it, do not allow them to stop you from experiencing the blessing God has given you. If you will give yourself to the Holy Spirit and learn all you can; if you are willing to step out and risk being wrong; if you will submit to the process and receive correction from the Spirit and those around you—you are a good candidate for being used powerfully in this gift of prophecy.

When we receive the gift of prophecy, then we need to learn how to steward it. A big part of that is encapsulated in the previous two chapters in this book. As we diligently study the written Word of God and spend time with the Lord, learning to know His heart, we will mature in the gift. In the Kingdom, the gifts are never intended to exist apart from relationship, thus one of the main ways we grow in the spiritual gifts is through developing our relationship with God. As we diligently steward the gift through time with God and in His Word, we will be prepared to operate in the gift when we are with others.

Another extremely practical way to grow in the gift of prophecy is to use it. Romans 12:8 says we prophesy in proportion to our faith. When we are obedient to say what we believe He is telling us, we can receive feedback from others and grow in our confidence. The only way we will ever know if the word we think we have received is encouraging or comforting is if we share it with the person or group we believe it's for. This, of course, is a risk. And it can feel scary. But the more we practice, the more we will be able to discern what we're hearing from God and how best to deliver it.

Now, let's look at the third line on the prophetic pyramid—the calling of the office of the prophet, which is given to some believers.

Some - Prophets

A person who has been given the gift of prophecy by the Holy Spirit (see 1 Cor. 12:10) is not the same as the person (prophet) who is an actual gift given by the Lord Jesus Christ to the body of Christ. In Ephesians 4:11–12, Paul lists what is often called the fivefold ministries or gifts to the Church:

> *So Christ himself gave the apostles, the prophets, the evangelists, the pastors and teachers, to equip his people for works of service, so that the body of Christ may be built up until we all reach unity in the faith and in the knowledge of the Son of God and become mature, attaining to the whole measure of the fullness of Christ* (Ephesians 4:11–13).

In other words, those called to these five offices in the Church are a gift from God to the Church for the purpose of bringing the Church to maturity and unity. Paul also mentions these callings in First Corinthians: *"God has placed in the church first of all apostles, second prophets, third teachers..."* (1 Cor. 12:28). These callings operated in the New Testament Church—*"Now in the church at Antioch there were certain prophets and teachers..."* (Acts 13:1)—and they continue to exist today.

A simple way to distinguish between the person who has the gift of prophecy and the person who is called as a prophet is this:

- One is given a gift—the gift of prophecy
- The other *is* the gift that is given—the office of prophet

It is important to note that people who have been called to the office of prophet may not yet be recognized as such because they are still in the process of maturing or because the assembly they are part of does not understand these teachings in the Scriptures. True prophets may recognize their calling but will wait and allow others to confirm and establish that calling. The calling will manifest itself, and God will eventually cause others to recognize it.

All the principles we discussed related to the person who has the gift of prophecy also apply to the person who is called to the office of prophet. Prophets should always be subject to both the Scriptures and the leaders in a local assembly. Ideally, they should be part of a local assembly where their ministry can be recognized and held accountable. Within that assembly, they should be leading and training others to operate in the prophetic. They should also receive the mind of the Lord and prophesy. In other words, they should be entering in themselves, as well as equipping others to enter in and do the work of the ministry. They will look for opportunities to call forth God's gifts in the saints. They are able to see already existing gifts in people, as well as impart gifts to them (see 1 Tim. 4:14; 2 Tim. 1:6). This description shows us the three main functions of someone called to the office of prophet:

1. Equipping the body (see Eph. 4:11–12)
2. Prophesying
3. Imparting the gift of prophecy to others (see Rom. 1:11; 1 Tim. 4:14; 2 Tim. 1:6)

Prophets do not just prophesy. They also impart and equip, and that is part of what sets those called as prophets apart from those who have the gift of prophecy. The same is true of the other fivefold office's of apostle, evangelist, pastor, and teacher. They have a unique calling to equip the body of Christ into maturity and unity.

Sometimes people ask how prophecy can be taught. (Or they say it *cannot* be taught!) This question is most likely rooted in the belief that if prophecy is really from the Holy Spirit and is really supernatural, it should not need to be taught. Instead, the prophetic word should come upon a person almost against that person's will. This is how some people perceive prophecy, but it is not a biblical view. Instead, like the other gifts of the spirit, prophecy is a partnership between us and God. When He gives us a gift, He gives us a particular faculty in that area; then we are responsible to learn how to partner with His Spirit to use it to our greatest capacity. Those who have the gift of evangelism need practice and instruction to maximize their gift most effectively. The same is true of prophecy. This is where those who hold the office of prophet come in. They teach others how to maturely use the gift of prophecy and the spirit of prophecy.

The apostle Paul, as a fivefold minister, emphasized the importance of teaching on the spiritual gifts when he wrote, *"Now about the gifts of the Spirit, brothers and sisters, I do not want you to be uninformed"* (1 Cor. 12:1). He did not want them to be in the dark, without teaching, or to have any misunderstanding about any of the spiritual gifts, including prophecy. He wanted the subject comprehensively taught. Paul knew everyone needed to be taught about the supernatural gifts because he knew the value of having these gifts functioning in the body of Christ. The gifts are not just "extras" that we can choose to do without. They are vital, living necessities to keep us growing and thriving daily. And the office of the prophet is essential to our ability to learn and thrive.

The Ongoing Need for Prophets in the Church

While some Christians believe the gifts of the Spirit ceased after the first century, the Bible makes it clear that we have an ongoing need for each of these gifts and callings, including the office of the prophet. Ephesians 4:13 says the fivefold offices will continue to exist *"until we all reach unity in the faith and in the knowledge of the Son of God and become mature, attaining to the whole measure of the fullness of Christ."* We all know this has not yet happened! Instead, a great deal of disunity of faith and heart exists among the members of the body of Christ. We still have a great need for these fivefold ministry men and women, including prophets.

Further, prophets also play an important role in God's communication with His Church regarding His plans on earth. The Bible tells us prophets always see what God is doing first and ahead of time. *"Surely the Sovereign LORD does nothing without revealing his plan to his servants the prophets"* (Amos 3:7). God is in partnership with us, as His people, and He uses the prophets as His messengers to tell us His plans so we can participate with them. Because He will not move without the cooperation of His Church, New Covenant prophetic ministry is very important to the advancing of God's Kingdom on earth.

Also, we can gather from several New Testament warnings against false apostles and false prophets (see 2 Cor. 11:13; Rev. 2:2; 2 Pet. 2:1; 1 John 4:1) that the fivefold offices continue in importance. Otherwise, such warnings would not be necessary. If prophets and apostles no longer existed, we wouldn't need to be warned about imposters.

Of course, on the opposite end of the spectrum from those who don't believe in prophets are those who put too much weight on specific prophetic words. Many who receive a prophetic word from someone accept it as if it's final in and of itself. They treat it like a direct and infallible word from the mouth of God. This is also an imbalanced perspective, as no prophet prophesies perfectly. This is why God tells us in the Bible to test every word and keep what is good. He has put the responsibility to test prophetic words on us, and He will hold us accountable for what we do or don't do with those things spoken to us.

The reality is, *"We know in part, and we prophesy in part"* (1 Cor. 13:9). God Himself speaks perfectly and without flaws, but our hearing skills are imperfect. When we hear from God, the words must pass through the filter of our own understanding, past experiences, present situations, emotional experiences, hurts, knowledge, and training. God has to first speak to the person delivering the prophecy; then the person releases the word. In this way, it passes through the prophet's filter before it arrives at the recipient's filter.

Testing prophecies just makes sense. If we don't, we risk falling prey to someone's cloudy filter, which could make all the difference in our ability to rightly understand what God is saying. When First Thessalonians 5:20–22 tells us, *"Do not treat prophecies with contempt but test them all; hold on* [tightly] *to what is good, reject every kind of evil,"* it is not just presenting a good idea but giving a directive. You test all things, check them out, ponder them, search them out, and examine them thoroughly. Then, hang on ever so tightly to what you have determined is good. We will discuss how to test a prophetic word in more detail in a later chapter.

Now let's examine the pinnacle of the prophetic pyramid—the Scriptures.

None - Scripture

The Scriptures, as a prophetic source of God's words to humanity, stand alone at the top of the pyramid. Nothing compares to them. They were originally inspired (or breathed) by God, and they have been confirmed as divine revelation throughout history. About them, the apostle Peter also wrote:

> *We also have the **prophetic message as something completely reliable**....Above all, you must understand that no prophecy of Scripture came about by the prophet's own interpretation of things. For prophecy never had its origin in the human*

> *will, but prophets, though human, spoke from God as they were carried along by the Holy Spirit* (2 Peter 1:19–21).

"The prophetic Scriptures" are the absolute *"sure word of prophecy"* (Rom. 16:26 NKJV; 2 Pet. 1:19 KJV). In Bible times, the Holy Spirit came upon particular men at particular times, and they wrote the message down (or had a scribe write it for them). What they received at those times was uniquely perfect, without human error. Now, in the New Covenant, the Holy Spirit no longer comes upon people, but if we are believers, He lives inside us. As a result, His ability to speak through us is confined to our person and our willingness to be used. His words through us are not perfect like the words of the prophets who experienced the Holy Spirit coming upon them.

These four types of prophetic ability (the Spirit of prophecy, the gift of prophecy, prophets, and Scripture) show us who can prophesy and the limits to that prophecy. In this blessed season in history, we all may prophesy by the Spirit of God!

The Revelation Gifts

In First Corinthians 12–14 we find the most detailed instruction on the gifts or various manifestations of the Holy Spirit. Here we learn that *"to each one the manifestation of the Spirit is given for the common good"* (1 Cor. 12:7). The Holy Spirit works with and through us as individuals; as a result, a wide range of activities is possible in the use of these gifts, and the various gifts can be expressed in many different ways. He has given His children a beautiful amount of freedom as we work in cooperation with Him.

In chapter 12, we find the well-known list of nine specific spiritual gifts:

- word of wisdom
- word of knowledge
- faith
- gifts of healings
- working of miracles
- prophecy

- discerning of spirits
- various kinds of tongues
- interpretation of tongues

These nine gifts have been categorized as **signs** (tongues and interpretation); **revelation gifts** (prophecy, word of wisdom, word of knowledge, and discerning of spirits); and **power gifts** (faith, healings, miracles). In this chapter, we will take a closer look at the revelation gifts.

Prophecy

First, let's look at the gift of prophecy (see 1 Cor. 12:10). The realm of the Holy Spirit is a prophetic realm. It is the channel through which the other gifts can function freely. Think of it as a piece of PVC pipe used in plumbing, with various other lines feeding into the main line. It is the vessel through which the heart and mind of God can be expressed. Often when a person begins to function in the prophetic, the other revelation gifts will begin to crisscross throughout a time of ministry. The word *prophecy* can be explained several ways. It means "to speak forth or flow forth." It can bubble up like an artesian well. It can announce something and/or speak for God. It is divinely inspired speech. It may be a declaration. When we as God's people learn to quiet our souls and tune our spirits into what the Holy Spirit wants to say to us and others around us, we can become vessels through whom God can speak His prophetic words. We tune into the spiritual realm, become aware of God's heart and mind for a particular person or body of believers, and yield our minds and tongues to His use. In this way, we enable Him to share His thoughts with people.

Psalm 139:17–18 says, *"How precious to me are your thoughts, God! How vast is the sum of them! Were I to count them, they would outnumber the grains of sand…."* Since the Lord has this many thoughts about any one person at any one time, we can ask Him to share just one of those thoughts with us so we can pass it on and encourage, comfort, or exhort someone. This is a simple way to understand and to enter into prophecy.

We find a perfect example of the use of prophecy in Isaiah 50:4, which says, *"The Sovereign LORD has given me a well-instructed tongue, to know the word that sustains the weary."* When another person needs encouragement, comfort, or exhortation to action, we can be the vessel God uses to speak right to that person's heart. How wonderful it would be if this gift functioned in every local church around the world! When anyone among us became weary, we could be the ones to lift that person up, to make that person feel important and useful again, to help that person find a place of belonging and service, and to give that person the confidence needed to fulfill God's calling! This is why it is so vital to have all of God's people moving in prophecy!

Unfortunately, some Christians have a hard time embracing spiritual realities because they are unseen with our natural eyes. However, the Bible tells us we must live by faith and not by sight (see 2 Cor. 5:7). This is crucial to the gift of prophecy because, as Romans 12:6 says, we prophesy according to our faith. In other words, we will be able to hear God's voice to the degree we believe we can. For this reason, we need to set aside our unbelief, agree with the Scriptures, and enter in by faith. This is the same kind of faith we use to receive salvation, speak in tongues, heal the sick, and experience all other spiritual realities (see Gal. 3:2).

When we begin to prophesy, we need to believe that when we ask the Lord to share His thoughts with us regarding a particular person and a thought or picture or song comes to mind, it is His answer to us. People spend too much time second guessing themselves and what they hear. *Is this the Lord? Or is it me?* This is a frustrating and self-defeating cycle. Instead, you need to trust that if you have asked Him He is faithful and will answer you. He's been known to do that! You ask and He answers; when you speak what you hear, the other person is blessed. (See Luke 11:11–13.) We know He wants us to be involved in blessing others, so we can trust He will be willing to share with us for that purpose. When we ask Him to give us a prophetic word, we need to dare to trust Him and receive what comes to us as being from Him. And we need to be faithful to share whatever He tells us, no matter how small or insignificant it might seem to us. We don't know the other person like the Father does. We don't know what that person needs to hear the way the Father does. Instead, we get to take a risk and share what we hear, trusting God to make the meaning and significance clear to that person's heart.

I heard the story of a young woman who was chosen to sit in a chair in the front of a prophecy class. Everyone else was to ask the Lord for something He wanted to say to bless her. A man came from the back row and began to sing to her the familiar little tune, "You are My Sunshine." After he sang it through once, he sang it again. He felt sort of foolish, as he didn't know what this would have to do with anything, but he shared what he had received faithfully. By the time he was done, the young woman had tears running down her face. She then shared that her own natural father had just recently passed away, and he used to sing that song to her every night at bedtime while she was growing up. This was God's way of saying to her that even though her natural father was no longer with her, He was her Father, and He would sing that song to her. What a powerful and timely message! If the man had not taken the risk and sung the song, the message from God to the young woman would have not been delivered, and she would not have experienced a revelation of God's knowledge of the personal details of her life and care for her in the midst of her grief. Truly, healthy prophetic ministry within the body of Christ is so vital to our wellbeing and maturity.

When we are ministering prophetically, it is important to remember that it is never our responsibility to make sure a word we deliver comes to pass. We are only to give it as clearly, carefully, and faithfully as we possibly can. Then we leave it to God and the person receiving it. The prophet Jeremiah said God watches over His word to perform it: *"The LORD said to me, 'You have seen correctly, for I am watching to see that my word is fulfilled'"* (Jer. 1:12). At another place, Jeremiah said, *"Amen! May the LORD do so! May the LORD fulfill the words you have prophesied..."* (Jer. 28:6). If the words we speak are truly from the Lord, He will bring them to pass in cooperation with the person who received them. If they are not from Him, they will come to nothing. He is only obligated to carry out His own word, not ours.

When we are delivering a message from the Lord to someone, we are just the messengers, not the enforcers. We submit the message in the very best way we can, and then we leave it with the person. Delivery is our responsibility. Testing and action on the message is the receiver's responsibility. It is always good to remember that we could be wrong. None of us hears perfectly or delivers perfectly. A good dose of humility will go a long way in helping us prophesy in a way that will truly bless and empower others. In the next chapter, we will talk about specific ways we can receive prophetic words.

The Word of Knowledge

Second, we come to the gift of the word of knowledge (see 1 Cor. 12:8). Simply put, it is a word of insight or a supernatural knowledge of specific information, facts, dates, times, or experiences in the past or the present.

Knowledge is defined as "learning or familiarity gained through experience or study." When we receive a word of knowledge, we receive information from God that we are not at all acquainted with and would have no natural way of knowing. This knowledge does not come from study or from acquiring information through our minds. It comes directly into our spirits from the mind and heart of God. And it is for the purpose of restoration and redemption.

The word of knowledge is very helpful in connection with the gifts of healing and working of miracles. The Spirit often will reveal to someone that a person has a particular need for healing or a miracle. It may be as simple as a body part, such as a knee or a shoulder. The person receiving the word of knowledge may experience temporary pain or tightness or numbness in that particular body part, showing the need of the person coming for prayer. The sensation may be very brief or may last for a while; therefore, the person operating in the word of knowledge for healing must pay close attention to what is happening in his or her own body. This, however, is only one way of receiving the word of knowledge for healing. We may also hear a sound, see words over the person, see a particular body part, know in our spirit what happened to cause the physical problem, or any other number of possibilities.

This can be quite scary to step out in, but you won't know if you're getting it right unless you try. The best approach, for beginners, is to ask questions. If you think you are receiving something from the Spirit, just say what you have and submit it to the person. For example, if you're feeling pain in your shoulder, you could ask, "Do you have pain in your shoulder?" The person can then answer you, and you can continue from there. Most likely you will be onto something, and the Spirit will use you to minister to the person. If the person says no and it really doesn't resonate with the person, apologize politely and say you're still learning. Please don't stop trying.

The first time I stepped out in a larger context with prophecy, the lady stopped me and kept repeating, "No, that's not it; no...no, that's not it." I did what I had been taught by my mentor in prophecy. I apologized and asked if I could pray for her. I left knowing in my heart I had gotten it right, but I didn't understand what had happened. A few nights later, the Lord justified me. The same woman came back to the meetings and shared about how she had a dream that reminded her of something she had forgotten. It was exactly what I had shared a few nights earlier, when she was so sure I had gotten it wrong. The moral of this story is, you should never withdraw and decide not step out again. Of course, you should never push prophetic words on people. It is not your job to make sure they receive it. Only God can do that. Your job is simply to share what you have heard and be respectful. As you step out and practice, you will learn and grow in your ability in this gift.

The Word of Wisdom

Third, let's look at the gift of the word of wisdom (see 1 Cor. 12:8). *Wisdom* is defined as "having or showing good sense." It is the ability to understand what is happening or will happen and to decide on the right course of action to take. A word of wisdom is a word of insight into the present or the future that you, as a human vessel, would have no way of knowing apart from supernaturally receiving it from the mind of the Spirit. It is different from good advice, although it will be that. It is specific advice, counsel, and direction for a specific situation. A word of wisdom will most likely have guidance included in it, because it is showing what should be done about something. It will most likely not seem as dramatic as a word of knowledge. A *word* implies a spoken message coming from the Holy Spirit, through a person, at a given moment. It is not an abiding deposit of wisdom from experience or age.

Paul wrote about the abundant wisdom of Jesus in Colossians 2:3: *"In whom* [Jesus] *are hidden all the treasure of wisdom and knowledge."* He knows what we need even when we do not. And He often releases wisdom for our difficult situations through another person operating in the gift of the word of wisdom. This is one more reason why it is so important to have a healthy, vibrant relationship with the Lord. When we do, we will be able to draw from His Spirit to meet the needs around us.

Discerning of Spirits

Fourth, we have the gift of discerning of spirits (see 1 Cor. 12:10). According to *Webster's New Collegiate Dictionary*, one definition of the word *discern* is "to come to know or understand the difference." The word *discernment* is defined as "the quality of being able to grasp and comprehend what is obscure." It is "a power to see what is not evident to the average mind." *The New Lexicon Webster's Dictionary* defines the word *discern* as "to see or make out through any of the senses...discrimination, insight, perception." The word *discerning* in the Greek (*diadrisis*) means "judging through." It means "distinguishing, determining clearly, piercing all that is merely outward, seeing right through and then forming a judgment based on that supernatural spiritual insight." Similarly, *The Complete Christian Dictionary for Home and School* says to *discern* means "to see, notice...to understand."

First John 4:1 admonishes us, *"Do not believe every spirit, but test the spirits to see whether they are from God..."* Here we see that the gift of discerning of spirits helps us distinguish what comes from God (and what does not). We are able to do this by receiving spiritual knowledge from the Holy Spirit. Discernment is not based in our human emotions or opinions. As First Corinthians 2:14 says, *"The person without the Spirit does not accept the things that come from the Spirit of God but considers them foolishness, and cannot understand them because they are discerned only through the Spirit."* True discernment will often seem like foolishness to our natural minds or emotions, but we are not discerning by them but by the Spirit.

This is why it is important to understand that the gift of discerning of spirits is not the same as a critical spirit in the natural. John Wesley once remarked that such a "talent" might well be buried without grieving the Lord at all. This "talent" refers to people who are adept at finding something wrong in the motives of other people. This is not discerning of spirits! It is being critical. There is also a natural instinct, sometimes known as "the sixth sense" or "woman's intuition." This is not the gift of discerning of spirits either! It is simply extra sensitivity and awareness in particular areas. Discerning of spirits only functions through the spirit of a person.

One of the ways this gift is used is in discerning evil. The fact that this gift exists at all presupposes the real existence of evil and deceiving spirits that manifest themselves through human beings. Of course, we do not need to be afraid of evil powers working around us, because the Bible tells us, *"The one who is in you is greater than the one who is in the world"* (1 John 4:4). He has given us the solution to the evil we see. The first step is recognizing it for what it is. Satan is persistently dogging the activities of the Holy Spirit and counterfeiting His works in order to deceive and work havoc among God's people. New converts come in who have been involved in all sorts of demonic activity and have not yet experienced deliverance. Even many long-time believers have never been delivered from their former activities. Often even human emotions and thoughts contradict the purposes of God. We see an example of this in Matthew 16:23: *"Jesus turned and said to Peter, 'Get behind me, Satan! You are a stumbling block to me; you do not have in mind the concerns of God, but merely human concerns.'"*

When we recognize evil, it is all too easy for us to respond in anger or judgment toward the spirit without having love and compassion for the person involved. Those who claim to possess the gift of discerning of spirits and exercise it need to have the love of God *"poured out into [their] hearts through the Holy Spirit"* (Rom. 5:5). They should not exercise the gift in a harsh or censoring way—but with great compassion and desire for redemption and restoration.

Contrary to what many people believe, the gift of discerning of spirits is not simply a safeguard against evil spirits. That is only part of the picture. *Discernment* does not carry a positive or negative connotation. The key is that it picks up on information that might not be otherwise obvious. Along these lines, in his helpful book on prophecy, *You May All Prophesy*, Steve Thompson writes:

> The word *spirit* can refer to any of the following in Scripture: angels, demons, the human spirit, the Holy Spirit, anointings, or the motivating influence of a person. Discerning of spirits, then, is the ability to recognize and distinguish between different types of spirits and anointings. For years this gift was thought to refer only to the ability to determine when someone had a demonic problem. But, this is only one aspect of the gift; it is not the full expression of discerning of spirits. It, also, can identify spiritual gifts and callings, or function like a word of knowledge in healing,

identify angelic activity, the state of someone's heart, or the specific purpose of the Lord's presence in a meeting.[3]

The sum of the matter is, we need this gift so we can know what is going on around us, whether good or bad. We need to pay attention to those "feelings" we have. They just may be the Holy Spirit trying to speak to us. Sometimes things just don't "feel" right, though our minds can't understand why. Often, this is a sign we're using the gift of discernment. The more we heed these senses, the more confidence we will gain and the more proficient we will become at responding to the Lord's gift of discernment. The Lord wants to communicate with His people on a regular basis, but we can hardly expect Him to keep talking to us if we aren't willing to pay attention and obey Him.

All four of these revelation gifts of the Spirit—prophecy, the word of knowledge, the word of wisdom, and discernment of spirits—are essential to healthy church life. Without them, we miss out on God's messages of edification, exhortation, and comfort, and we fail to understand what is happening in the spirit realm. With them, we can step into a fuller experience of the Christian life and all God has for us as His children.

Now that we've looked at the four revelations gifts, in the next chapter we will discuss how to function in the spiritual realm, including various ways people receive prophetic revelation.

six

Living in the Spirit Realm

According to *The New Bible Dictionary*, "The Greek idea of knowledge was a contemplation of reality in its *static* and *abiding* being." *Static*, as it is used here, means "unchanging." *Abiding* means "remaining, lasting, enduring." Thus, Greeks believed they could gain knowledge by observing material objects around them—what we might call "head knowledge" today. By contrast,

> The Hebrew was primarily concerned with life in its dynamic process; and therefore, they conceived knowledge as an entry into relationship with the experience world which makes demands not only on the understanding, but also on the will....This is what we call "heart knowledge." The criterion of this knowledge is obedience.[4]

In this difference between the Greek and Hebrew way of knowing, we find an explanation for what it means to know and experience in the spirit realm. This chapter is all about the experiential (heart) knowledge of God that is an essential part of learning to function in the spiritual realm. When we experience Him for ourselves, we become *convinced* of what we *know*. Thus, we will use the word *convinced* in reference to experiential knowledge.

In the Spirit and the Natural

We all belong to and live in dual realms simultaneously. We are physical, and we are spiritual. Our souls serve one or the other of these arenas. As Christians, we believe in and serve an invisible God who lives and reigns in an invisible Kingdom—the Kingdom of God. This realm is the source of all we see with our natural eyes. Thus, we must first receive in the invisible realm before we can pray and work in cooperation with God to bring things to pass in the physical world.

To function in both the spiritual and the natural realms, we must be like people who speak more than one language and are comfortable with more than one culture. Even within the United States, we live in many different regions where we are used to speaking and doing life a certain way. Some of us speak with a different accent and have a different culture, even though we speak the same language and live in the same country. The more easily we can put aside our own way of doing things and enter into something new, the more easily we can switch from one culture to another. This illustrates what it can be like going back and forth, so to speak, between the spirit realm and the natural realm.

Some people like to say, "That person is so heavenly-minded he is no earthly good." This is a misunderstanding. Instead, we need to be both heavenly-minded and earthly good. We need to be able to see into the spiritual realm and bring what we see into earthly existence. Heaven wants to bless earth and its inhabitants.

Why Faith Matters

Even though, as born-again Christians, our citizenship is in the spiritual realm, we usually feel more comfortable with this earthly realm. We are aware of the sights, sounds, feelings, smells, and activities of what is going on around us. We are not so aware of the same things in the spiritual realm. In fact, we are often uncomfortable and even fearful of spiritual things.

In our culture, we are continually inundated with the idea that "seeing is believing," and many Christians actually believe it is true! However, the Scriptures teach otherwise, as we see in the story of Thomas:

> ...He [Thomas] *said to them, "Unless I see the nail marks in his hands and put my finger where the nails were, and put my hand into his side, I will not believe."...Then he* [Jesus] *said to Thomas, "Put your finger here; see my hands. Reach out your hand and put it into my side. Stop doubting and believe." Thomas said to him, "My Lord and my God!" Then Jesus told him, "Because you have seen me, you have believed; blessed are those who have not seen and yet have believed"* (John 20:25–31).

Jesus identified Thomas' need to see in order to believe as weak and small faith, and He praised those who would believe in Him without seeing the physical evidence of His resurrection. Hebrews 11, the faith chapter, takes this idea ever farther. It tells us faith (belief in the unseen) is the basis for all that is done in the spiritual world:

> *Now faith is confidence in what we hope for and assurance about what we do not see. This is what the ancients were commended for. By faith we understand that the universe was formed at God's command, so that what is seen was not made out of what was visible* (Hebrews 11:1–3).

Here we learn that we see things in the spiritual *before* they appear in the natural. In the spiritual, we know they already exist; therefore, we make decisions and take actions based on what we know in our spirits, not on what we can see with our natural eyes. This is the definition of faith. The patriarchs, Noah and Abraham, both demonstrated this sort of faith:

> *By faith Noah, being divinely warned of things not yet seen, moved with godly fear, prepared an ark....By faith, Abraham obeyed when he was called to go out to the place which*

he would receive as an inheritance. And he went out, not knowing where he was going (Hebrews 11:7–8 NKJV).

Faith has a promise from God before it materializes into our temporal world. This spiritual reality is just as real *before* we see it in the natural as it is when it's in front of us. In a sense, faith is like bifocal glasses; it enables us to see up close things that are very far away. This is a great gift that can help us in so many ways in our lives. However, it also requires risk.

Hebrews 11:7 tells us Noah built the ark because he was moved by godly fear. He stepped out in faith because he feared God more than he feared what might happen if he had somehow heard God wrong. Unfortunately, unlike Noah, many of us are prevented from hearing God and obeying Him because of ungodly *fear*. Two kinds of fear have a part in our efforts to walk in faith. Godly fear, the kind Noah had, compels us to obey God above all others, no matter the cost. Ungodly fear, which is mentioned in 2 Timothy 1:7—*"God has not given us a spirit of fear, but of power and of love and of a sound mind"* (NKJV)—causes us to disobey God because we fear what will happen if we're wrong or we fear what others will think. Essentially, ungodly fear causes us to doubt the goodness and truthfulness of God, and that is a serious problem.

If we want to move in any of the gifts of the Spirit, we will face the choice of which fear to walk in. Too often, when the Spirit tries to speak to and through a person, that person is much more attentive to the voice of fear than to the voice of the Spirit. And that voice of fear causes paralysis. Instead, like Noah, we need to hear from God about *"things not yet seen"* and be moved with godly fear to obey His voice.

When others question or mock us because of our obedience, we need to reaffirm to ourselves that we have seen or heard or known something that is *"not yet seen"* with the natural eye. We need to encourage ourselves that we have a *"sound mind,"* and we're not losing it. And we need to continue with diligence to do what we believe He has spoken to us.

The Five Spiritual Senses

The ways God can speak to us are as numerous and varied as His children. Jesus said, His sheep know His voice (see John 10:4), which means all of us are prophetic. Every one of us has the ability to hear Him speak. And the prophet Amos tells us that prophecy is the natural outcome of hearing God's voice:

> *Surely the Lord God does nothing unless He reveals His secrets to His servants the prophets. A lion has roared! Who will not fear? The Lord God has spoken! Who can help but prophesy?* (Amos 3:7)

Just as fear follows the roaring of a lion, so prophecy follows the hearing of God's voice. It is the natural outcome. We can all prophesy.

Because God speaks in various ways through His Spirit (see Heb. 1:1), we must be very careful not to limit Him in *how* He speaks. Larry Randolph enumerates in his book, *Spirit Talk*, just a few ways God may try to speak to us. Among these he includes divine appearances; angels; visions; trances; dreams; audible voice; inner voice and conscience; intuition, perception and impressions; mental pictures; physical senses; nature; the cosmos; people; the secular world; coincidence and circumstances; and Scripture. The possibilities are endless! He can use situations, reading materials, road signs, clocks, television commercials, or anything else He wants to use.

Because of this, we must commit ourselves to tuning into the Spirit realm and seriously listening to what He might want us to understand. God spoke through a donkey when Balaam would not listen any other way (see Num. 22:22–31). Let's not force Him to go to such great lengths to share His heart with us. One way we can learn to enter into the ways of the Spirit is by turning to the Old Testament prophets, as well as the New Testament book of Revelation. As we read these books carefully, we will see there is so much more than what we have experienced. And some people will find validation for experiences they have had but didn't understand. These books show us the interactions of ordinary people (just like us) with the spirit realm, describing their interactions in terms of the five senses. The writers speak about seeing, hearing, smelling, tasting, and feeling.

When we understand that we live in parallel realms—spiritual and natural—we will understand that, in the same way that we have five physical senses to function in the natural realm, we also have five parallel spiritual senses that enable us to function in the spiritual realm. In the physical realm, we can know the pizza is ready for dinner by hearing the oven timer *ding*, by seeing the pizza with our eyes, by smelling the pizza, by touching the pizza, and finally by tasting the pizza. In the same way, God likes to use the various spiritual senses to communicate a message to us.

In the natural realm, we interact through our five senses and our minds. The same is true in the spiritual realm regarding the spiritual senses and revelation. Many people are fearful of "living by feelings," and as a result, they do not open themselves to spiritual experiences. However, if we are diligent to test everything against Scripture, we don't need to worry about this. God has already provided an anchor for us to keep us connected to the truth. We are not advocating "living by feelings" but experiencing all the Spirit has for us. We are advocating becoming completely comfortable in the spirit realm, to the point that we feel at home there. To be truly supernatural Christians, we need to be able to speak both languages (natural and spiritual). We need to be able to live and function in both cultures. The natural realm desperately needs to be changed by what Heaven has to say. In order to bring God's words to earth, we need to understand the language of Heaven so we can interpret it into earthly language.

Think how limited life would be if we were blind, deaf, paralyzed, and numb, if we had no taste buds or smelling ability! We would barely be able to function, let alone help anyone else! We would have to depend on others to take care of us for so many things. Yet in the Church, many people cannot spiritually see, hear, feel, or perceive what the Spirit is saying and doing in the heavenlies. We should not be OK with this.

Let's look at each of the five spiritual senses more closely.

Smelling

First, consider the sense of smell. Many of the biblical prophets used very descriptive language in an attempt to share their experiences with us in a way we can understand. Some describe what they received as something they saw or something they heard. The descriptive language used, especially in Isaiah and Revelation, causes us to wonder whether Isaiah and John could actually smell the fire they saw. In Isaiah 6:6, Isaiah mentions *"...a live coal...which he had taken with tongs from the altar...."* I believe Isaiah could smell that fire. When you walk down a street and smell what is cooking at a nearby restaurant or the smell of logs burning in a campfire or the smell of hot coals in a backyard barbecue grill, you are experiencing life with your senses in the natural realm. Isaiah, in a vision in the spiritual realm, could also experience with his senses all that was happening around him.

We see something similar in Revelation:

> *Another angel, who had a golden censer, came and stood at the altar. He was given much incense to offer, with the prayers of all God's people, on the golden altar in front of the throne* (Revelation 8:3).

I find it very difficult to think no smell came from that heavenly altar, that the "much incense" did not create a good bit of fragrance. How did John know the angel was given much incense? Perhaps he visually recognized what it was, or maybe it was mentioned verbally. Or perhaps he recognized it by its smell.

Tasting

Second, let's consider the sense of taste. We find the spiritual sense of taste explicitly mentioned in Ezekiel 2:9–3:3:

> *Then I looked, and I saw a hand stretched out to me. In it was a scroll, which he unrolled before me. On both sides of it were written words of lament and mourning and woe. And he [the Spirit] said to me, "Son of man, eat what is before you, eat this scroll; then go and speak to the people of Israel." So I opened my mouth, and he gave me the scroll to eat. Then he said to me, "Son of man, eat this scroll I am giving you and fill your stomach with it." So I ate it, and it tasted as sweet as honey in my mouth.*

The Spirit did not give Ezekiel natural food; it was symbolic. Yet he experienced the sense of taste in the spiritual as he symbolically ate the scroll. *"So I ate it, and it tasted as sweet as honey in my mouth."*

John the apostle had a mirror experience in Revelation 10:8–11:

> *Then the voice that I had heard from heaven spoke to me once more: "Go, take the scroll that lies open in the hand of the angel who is standing on the sea and on the land." So I went to the angel and asked him to give me the little scroll. He said to me, "Take it and eat it. It will turn your stomach sour, but 'in your mouth it will be as sweet as honey.'" I took the little scroll from the angel's hand and ate it. It tasted as sweet as honey in my mouth, but when I had eaten it, my stomach turned sour. Then I was told, "You must prophesy again about many peoples, nations, languages and kings."*

John, in the spirit, ate a scroll and experienced the sensations of a sweet taste in his mouth and a bitter feeling in his stomach. He spiritually experienced two very different tastes. John did not eat a literal book in the natural. If he had done that, it would have tasted like paper, and his stomach would have most likely become nauseous. Instead, he ate and tasted with his spiritual senses, and what he tasted (sweet and then bitter) had a prophetic meaning.

Seeing

Third is the sense of sight. When people see in the spirit, they will see things that are spiritual realities but not natural realities, and they will often be able to see them with their natural eyes. For example, they may see words above or on a person. Words that aren't there in the natural may appear on walls. When ministering in healing, one might see pictures of certain body parts, which are the parts needing healing. The ability to see in the spirit is important because God often speaks through pictures, symbols, types, and figures. Prophetic pictures and symbolic language are used throughout the Old Testament, and Jesus also used symbolic language and told symbolic stories (parables).

Many of the Old Testament prophets described their experiences from the Lord with visionary words like *saw, showed, vision,* and *looking*. The way they expressed what they received and how they received it tells us a lot about what spiritual senses they were using in their interaction with the spirit realm. For some of them, sight was one of their primary spiritual senses. God *"spoke to the prophets, gave them many visions and told parables through them"* (Hosea 12:10). Throughout the book of Amos, we read that Amos saw what God spoke to him (see Amos 1:1; 7:1, 4, 12–13; 8:1–2; 9:1). Obadiah's prophecy is called a vision (see Obad. 1:1). Micah also saw the word of the Lord (see Micah 1:1). Nahum and Habakkuk both saw a burden from the Lord (see Nah. 1:1; Hab. 1:1). Throughout Zechariah's book, he speaks of seeing and raising his eyes to look at the message from God (see Zech. 1:7–8, 18; 2:1, 3; 3:1; 4:1; 5:1, 5; 6:1). Two of the most famous Old Testament prophets, Isaiah and Jeremiah, also used visionary language in speaking about how God spoke to them (see Isa. 1:1; 2:1; 6:1; 13:1; Jer. 1:11, 13). They were all seer prophets.

First Samuel 9:9 gives us the term seer: *"Formerly in Israel, if someone went to inquire of God, they would say, 'Come, let us go to the seer,'* **because the prophet of today used to be called a seer."** A seer is simply a prophet who primarily receives prophetic revelation through seeing spiritual realities. When God shows us a picture or a color or a number, we must learn how to interpret what He is saying and put it into words so the people we are ministering to will be encouraged, exhorted, and comforted. If we cannot interpret what He is speaking to us, we are not able to take action on His words. This is one benefit of knowing what certain types and symbols generally stand for—especially biblically. (For the best book on the topic, read *The School of the Seers* by our son, Jonathan Welton)

Hearing

Fourth is the most common way of receiving information in the spirit—the sense of hearing. This can include hearing in the spirit and hearing with the physical ears. The Old Testament prophet Elijah heard with his natural ears the quiet voice of the Lord after hearing and experiencing other things (see 1 Kings 19:12–13). Many other Bible characters heard angels speak to them.

Some of the Old Testament prophets expressed what they received from the Lord in auditory language, saying things like, "*The word of the Lord came.*" The books of Zephaniah and Malachi both begin with a statement about the word of the Lord coming to the prophet (see Zeph. 1:1; Mal. 1:1). Likewise, throughout Haggai, we find references to hearing the word of the Lord (see Hag. 1:1, 3-11, 13; 2:1). Zechariah, too, often wrote that the word of the Lord came to him (see Zech. 1:1, 9; 7:4, 8; 8:1, 18; 9:1; 12:1). Jeremiah often heard the word of the Lord (see Jer. 1:4, 11, 13; 2:1; 11:1). And Daniel was told to seal up the words he'd heard for a later time period (see Dan. 12:4, 9).

One type of prophecy is called *nabi*. This refers to a sudden inspiration that comes upon a person with very little or no foreknowledge. When this happens to us, the prophetic word just suddenly bubbles up from deep within and "bursts" forth with inspiration. No pictures, colors, or numbers accompany *nabi* prophecy. We just open our mouths and begin to speak.

Feeling

Fifth, let's consider the sense of touch, or feeling. Simply put, the spiritual sense of feeling includes any physical sensation our bodies experience when we are in the manifest presence of God. These sensations can be prophetic, as with those who get words of knowledge for physical healing as pain in their bodies. The sensations can also simply be our bodies' responses to contact with the all-powerful God of the universe.

On several occasions, Daniel also experienced physical weakness due to the presence of God accompanying the visions he saw. He said, *"I had no strength left, my face turned deathly pale and I was helpless"* (Dan. 10:8). He also experienced something like a deep sleep on his face on the ground, trembling in his knees and hands, speechlessness, and loss of strength (see Dan. 10:9–11, 15–16). Fortunately, the angel who appeared to him strengthened him to be able to endure the presence of the Lord and hear the message (see Dan. 10:18–19).

In the New Testament, people responded in the same way when encountering a full manifestation of the presence of the Lord (see Matt. 28:2–4; Mark 16:5, 18; John 18:4–6). Even the apostle John, one of Jesus' closest friends during His life on earth, *"fell at his feet as though dead"* (Rev. 1:17) when the risen Christ appeared to him in all His glory.

In these five senses we see the vast array of ways in which God can and does speak to His people. Often, people will have one main way of receiving, but ideally, they will be able to function in several others as well. God wants us to be open to receiving from Him in any way He chooses to speak. We must never try to contain God or limit Him but instead allow Him to be God and choose to work with Him, no matter what He decides to do. The more we make ourselves available and step out into new opportunities, the more we will grow in our spiritual senses and in our prophetic ability. When we are fully awakened in our spiritual senses to the Spirit of the Lord, we will be open to receive and be aware of all that is taking place around us in the spirit realm.

seven

Rhythm and Rhyme

The phrase *rhythm and rhyme* refers to a pattern of rhymes created by using words that make the same or similar sounds. In writing (especially in poetry), it refers to the recurrence of similar sounds that results in a musical, gentle effect. Simply put, it is when the sounds of the words create a beautiful feel that complements the meaning and makes it easy to hear. Sometimes, God uses a similar effect with prophecy. Prophecy carries specific purposes for our lives. It is a serious and powerful matter. Yet often He clothes this serious business in beauty, in an art form that woos us with its loveliness and leaves a lasting impression on our hearts and minds. In this way, we sometimes experience prophecy in a way that transcends our words and understanding.

In this chapter, we will highlight some of the specific purposes of prophecy—what it does in our lives. Then we will look at some of the ways prophetic words are expressed—the way they dress up for the occasion.

What Prophecy Does

As we examine the purposes of prophecy, it is important to remember that God often sees things differently than we do. He is often more interested in the bigger picture than in the circumstance we are facing. His viewpoint is broad and all-encompassing. But we, many times, are consumed with the struggles of our daily lives. Since He knows all things can be worked together for good on our behalf, He may talk to us about something that seems to have nothing to do with our concern. He doesn't do this because He doesn't know about it or care about it; He is well aware of every detail of our lives, but He sees things differently than we do. Because of this, we need to walk in faith and trust in His goodness, even when we don't see the way ahead of us clearly. We can know He does see it, and He is working for our good, not only in our outward circumstances but also in our inner maturity.

With this in mind, let's examine some of the primary purposes of prophecy under the New Covenant. Each one of these purposes must align with the general standard of edification, exhortation, or comfort (see 1 Cor. 14:3 NKJV). If they do not, they are not conveying the heart of God and, therefore, should not be received.

1. Personal Strengthening

One of the primary purposes of prophecy is for personal encouragement and strengthening (see Judg. 7:7). God speaks to remind you of His provision and comfort in your life (see 1 Kings 3:5; Zech. 10:2). Through prophecy, He reveals more of His nature and character to you in order to bring you into a closer relationship with Him (see Num. 12:6; Dan. 2:47).

2. Direction

A prophecy may bring direction or instruction in your life (see Gen. 31:11–13, 24, 29; Job 33:14; Matt. 27:19).

3. Everyday Revelation

A prophecy can be a tremendous asset in everyday life as you interact with others. It can help you see and understand things the way God does. That, in turn, may radically change how you choose to deal with certain people and situations.

4. A Creative Word

A prophecy may be a creative word that begins something new in your life, something that was not previously in existence. This usually comes in the form of a declaration.

5. The Stirring Up of Gifts

A prophecy may call forth the gifts God has already placed in you. You may not have been aware of them before, and they were dormant within you. But the prophetic word activates them.

6. Impartation of Gifts

A prophecy may also be used to impart spiritual gifts to you that you did not previously have. We find an example of this in Paul's exhortation to his spiritual son, Timothy: *"For this reason I remind you to fan into flame the gift of God, which is in you through the laying on of my hands* (2 Tim. 1:6). Paul also told the Roman Christians, *"I long to see you so that I may impart to you some spiritual gift to make you strong"* (Rom. 1:11).

7. Insight for Healing

A prophecy may provide helpful insight when you are praying for physical and emotional healing. Through a prophetic word, God may highlight the root of the issue that, when addressed in prayer, will bring freedom and healing.

8. Salvation

A prophecy may reveal the thoughts and feelings in unbelievers' hearts and aid in bringing them to repentance. Paul mentions this when he writes:

But if an unbeliever or an inquirer comes in while everyone is prophesying, they are convicted of sin and are brought under judgment by all, as the secrets of their hearts are laid bare. So they will fall down and worship God, exclaiming, "God is really among you!" (1 Corinthians 13:24–25).

9. Revelation of the Future

The Bible is full of stories of prophecies that revealed the future, and God still uses prophecy in this way today.

10. Warning

A prophecy can also warn you of the enemy's plans and enable you to prevent or counteract them (see Gen. 20:3; Matt. 27:19).

11. Confirmation

A prophecy may also confirm something God has already spoken to you. Some people believe this is the sole function of prophecy, but this idea does not exist in Scripture. Prophecies do sometimes confirm what God has already said, but that is not the main purpose of the gift of prophecy.

In these eleven purposes we see God's desire to pour out His abundant blessing upon His people. He does not want us to wander aimlessly; He wants us to be people of vision who are led by His voice.

Now let's look at some of the ways prophecy is expressed, at the rhythm and rhyme.

What Prophecy Looks Like

We have a tendency to think of prophecy as being confined to the spoken word, but prophecy can actually be expressed in many different ways. An *expression* is something that manifests, embodies, or symbolizes something else. The idea behind prophetic expression is to see or hear what is taking place in the spirit realm and use some means in our natural realm to express the prophetic unction in a way that others can experience and understand. This is the power of prophetic rhythm and rhyme. God desires so much for us to understand what He is saying. When we act on His words, He is willing to speak in many different ways. Hebrews 1:1 says God spoke to the fathers in time past in various times and in various ways. We will cover some of those ways in this section.

Visual Art as Prophecy

According to the dictionary, *art* is "the conscious use of skill and creative imagination." God is the great artist of history, the creator of all. And when we create artistically, we do it through the creativity He has planted within us. God so values prophetic art that the first person the Bible mentions as being filled with the Spirit was the artist who created the tabernacle. About this man, Bezalel, God said:

> *I have filled him with the Spirit of God, with wisdom, with understanding, with knowledge, and with all kinds of skills— to make artistic designs for work in gold, silver and bronze, to cut and set stones, to work in wood, and to engage in all kinds of crafts* (Exodus 31:3–5).

God also filled a man named Oholiab with the Spirit so he could assist Bezalel in the creating of the tabernacle and instruct others in all kinds of artistic skills, including working with precious metals, setting precious stones, carving wood, engraving, designing, embroidering, and weaving (see Exod. 35:30–35; 38:23). In this example we see that God does, in fact, use art to convey prophetic messages.

Writing as Prophecy

Prophecy is often expressed through the written word. God told Moses to write down a song and teach it to the Israelites as a prophetic witness regarding what the Israelites would do in the future (see Deut.

31:19). Similarly, God told Ezekiel to write down a description of the temple He had shown him in a vision so he could show it to the Israelites (see Ezek. 43:11). The prophet Isaiah had this interesting experience:

> *The LORD said to me, "Take a large scroll and write on it with an ordinary pen: Maher-Shalal-Hash-Baz." So I called in Uriah the priest and Zechariah son of Jeberekiah as reliable witnesses for me. Then I made love to the prophetess, and she conceived and gave birth to a son. And the LORD said to me, "Name him Maher-Shalal-Hash-Baz. For before the boy knows how to say 'My father' or 'My mother,' the wealth of Damascus and the plunder of Samaria will be carried off by the king of Assyria"* (Isaiah 8:1–4).

Here there was special significance to the word being written and witnessed prior to the events it foretold. Isaiah also records a prophetic writing from King Hezekiah, after the Lord healed him (see Isa. 38). One of the most well-known verses related to written prophecy is in Habakkuk 2:2, "*Write down the revelation and make it plain on tablets so that a herald may run with it.*" The apostle John, too, was commanded to write down his prophecy contained in the Book of Revelation: "*Write on a scroll what you see…*" (Rev. 1:11). About this written prophecy, John said, "*Blessed is the one who reads aloud the words of this prophecy, and blessed are those who hear it and take to heart what is written in it* (Revelation 1:3).

Even God Himself once wrote a prophetic word on a wall with His own hand, which Daniel had to interpret for the Babylonian king, as it was written in a heavenly language (see Dan. 5). Clearly, the written word is a very common expression of prophecy.

Dance as Prophecy

Throughout the Bible, dance is often used as a prophetic expression. Some dances express celebration and victory, like Miriam's dance and song following the Lord's victory for Israel at the Red Sea (see Exod.

15:20–21). After David killed Goliath, his victory was celebrated in a dance and song comparing David to King Saul and implicitly prophesying David's future succession of Saul as king.

> *But the servants of Achish said to him, "Isn't this David, the king of the land? Isn't he the one they sing about in their dances: 'Saul has slain his thousands, and David his tens of thousands'?"* (1 Samuel 21:11).

Dance also often expresses love and joy. In Lamentations, we see the connection between dancing and joy. *"Joy is gone from our hearts; our dancing has turned to mourning"* (Lam. 5:15). The prophet Jeremiah likewise prophesied of a time when Israel would be rebuilt, and therefore, the people would dance again:

> *I will build you up again, and you, Virgin Israel, will be rebuilt. Again you will take up your timbrels and go out to dance with the joyful* (Jeremiah 31:4).

Ultimately, as an expression of praise to the Lord, prophetic dance uses the whole body to exult the King of kings. Such dancing was a normal part of Israel's devotional life, as we see in several of the psalms, which encourage the people to *"Praise his name with dancing and make music to him with timbrel and harp"* (Ps. 149:3), and *"Praise him with timbrel and dancing, praise him with the strings and pipe"* (Ps. 150:4).

Dance is a beautiful and powerful expression of the Spirit of God within us and can be used to release God's word over individuals and groups of people. The modern Church has often avoided dance as an act of worship, for fear of impurity, but the Bible makes it clear that dance is an important part of devotional life for all of us. Since David, as a man and warrior king, danced before the Lord with all his might, wearing just a linen ephod, a simple undergarment (see 2 Sam. 6:14), we can see the significance and purity of dance that honors and releases God's word.

Instrumental Music as Prophecy

Music is a powerful medium, whether it is accompanied by words or not, that draws us into the presence of God and releases His prophetic word—through sound—into the earth. We see this most in the life of the great worshiper, David. He witnessed the power of anointed music when he played his lyre for the tormented King Saul (see 1 Samuel 16:14–23). When he became king, because he understood the prophetic potential in music, David *"set apart some of the sons of Asaph, Heman and Jeduthun for the ministry of prophesying, accompanied by harps, lyres and cymbals..."* (1 Chron. 25:1–3). In this way, instrumental music can serve as a prophetic expression of God's desires and purposes.

Props, Actions, Drama, and Gestures as Prophecy

These expressions of a message from the Spirit can be summed up as the use of physical objects or symbolic actions to illustrate a message. They are simply props used to convey a particular point, and when it comes to prophecy, God is fond of using such props to embody His messages. The Old Testament prophet Ezekiel is particularly well-known for the use of props and actions to display to Israel what God wanted them to understand. Many of the messages Ezekiel delivered to Israel were acted out as skits or short dramas (see Ezek. 4–5). Such actions can make a message come alive and be more understandable.

Jeremiah also employed this method when God told him, *"Stand at the gate of the LORD's house and there proclaim this message"* (Jer. 7:1). Here the illustration is the place where the prophet stood when he announced the word of the Lord. Another time, God told him, *"Go and buy a linen belt and put it around your waist, but do not let it touch water"* (Jer. 13:1). In this case, this sash served as a symbol to make His point more tangible and impactful to His people. Similarly, Amos was told to *"strike the tops of the pillars so that the thresholds shake..."* (Amos 9:1) as an illustration of what the Lord was about to do. The prophet Hosea had to marry a harlot and father children with her as an illustration to Israel of how God saw them and their unfaithfulness to Him.

Sometimes God even told His prophets to prophesy against inanimate objects that symbolized a living reality. For example, He told Ezekiel to prophesy against the mountains of Israel (see Ezek. 6:1–2). Obviously, the mountains themselves had not done anything wrong. They simply served as a metaphor for the nation of Israel. Similarly, God told an unnamed man of God to prophesy against an altar at one of the high places of Israel (not in the temple), prophesying the judgment that would come because the people worshipped at the high places (see 1 Kings 13:2). Again, the altar was symbolic of the sinful actions of the people.

Jesus also used many natural illustrations, called parables, to help people understand what He meant. The phrase, *"The kingdom of heaven is like..."* occurs over and over throughout the gospels. In Acts 21:10–11, the prophet Agabus prophesied what would happen to Paul by using Paul's belt as a visual aid.

The props, actions, dramas, and gestures that God can use as prophetic acts or symbols are infinite. Images and actions are powerful communication tools, and God loves to use them in His communication with His people. He loves to use parts of our everyday lives to illustrate His messages, making them easier for us to comprehend.

eight

Stewarding Your Personal Prophetic Words

We've mentioned several times the importance of testing prophetic words. In this chapter, we will talk in greater depth about how to do that. I also want to highlight the importance of our role in the fulfillment of our prophetic words. The two ideas go hand-in-hand. And the moral of the story is that prophecy is not like some sort of magic incantation that causes what it declares apart from any human involvement. Instead, our involvement in the testing and fulfillment of our personal prophetic words is crucial.

Cooperating with God

In his first letter to Timothy, Paul counseled him regarding the prophetic word he had received:

> *Until I come, devote yourself to the public reading of Scripture, to preaching and to teaching. Do not neglect your gift, which was given you through prophecy when the body of elders laid their hands on you. Be diligent in these matters; give yourself wholly to them, so that everyone may see your progress* (1 Timothy 4:13–15).

Here we see the responsibility we have to partner with prophetic words once we receive them. We must not neglect the words we receive. We cannot just expect them to come to pass simply because they were spoken. Personal prophecies given through human vessels must always be tested, and we must cooperate with God to bring them to pass. They only speak to our potential.

We see an example of this in Judges 6:12, where the Angel of the Lord appeared to Gideon and said, *"The Lord is with you, mighty warrior!"* At the moment this word of the Lord came to Gideon, he was about as far away from being a mighty warrior as one could be. Rather, he was fearfully hiding from his enemies. God had spoken to Gideon's potential. Yet when Gideon heard the word, he had no understanding of it and did not respond to it with faith. He only looked at himself and his circumstances through his natural eyes, so he began to make excuses about why this word could not be correct. Everything around him seemed to contradict the word because the word spoke to his potential, not his current experience.

Here we see the importance of responding to the word of the Lord with faith. Without faith, our eyes will remain closed. We will not be good ground that receives the word of the Lord and allows it to grow and bring forth the fruit it is meant to yield. Here is an important key to understanding prophecy. We cannot mix our human understanding and reasoning together with the words of the Spirit to us. His words are meant to be received by faith. When we receive them by faith and act accordingly, the words will bear fruit in our lives, moving us from where we were to the place of our potential the word prophesied. When God looked at Gideon, He saw Gideon as a mighty warrior, but for that to become a reality in the natural realm, Gideon had to receive the word by faith and begin to step into that identity. He had to get past all the reasons why he couldn't possibly be a mighty warrior. He had to lay aside all his arguments and chose to agree with God that he, indeed, was a mighty warrior who could accomplish what God had called him to do.

Like Gideon, we too need to realize prophetic words contain life and have the power to bring forth Gods purposes—but they must be mixed with faith and action. Until we perceive it is the Lord speaking to us, the word will lay dormant (see Judg. 6:22). And it is possible for a genuine word from God to go completely unfulfilled, unless we receive it by faith and enter into partnership with Him. When the word was spoken to Gideon, it was true, but it did not *become* true until Gideon believed and acted on it. No matter how long a seed lays on a shelf, it contains within it the life needed to bring forth fruit. But it will never bring forth that fruit unless someone believes it is a seed, plants it in the soil, and tends it. The same is true of prophecy. It is not unconditional. Instead, it is God's invitation to see and understand things as He does, to enter into realities that we have not yet grasped. For this reason, when He speaks, we must agree with Him and ask Him to help us become all He has created us to be.

Imagine, for a moment, that you are a receiver on an American football team, and God is the quarterback. His job is to throw the ball to you; your job is to catch the ball and run with it toward the end zone (goal) in order to score points. If God throws you the ball, but you do nothing and let the ball fall to the ground, the reception will be unsuccessful. The same applies to prophecy. Often when people receive a personal prophetic word, they become very excited about what God said, but they don't understand the need to test the word. And they don't realize they must take action on the word (assuming it passed the tests). If they do not test the word and then become actively involved with it, that word may just sit there year after year and never come to pass. This, of course, may bring disappointment, discouragement, and even disbelief in prophecy. This is a sad scenario that happens way too often, all because of a lack of instruction.

Now consider the opposite scenario as an American football player. When God throws the ball to you, now you reach out to catch it. Once you have it safely in your hands, you begin to run. And you run all the way to the end of the field, where you cross the goal line and score a touchdown. At every step, you have the choice to stop. You can stop because you're too tired, your feet hurt, or you're simply bored with running. Or you can choose to hold the ball tightly and run straight forward to the goal line to make the touchdown. Situations in life have a way of sapping our energy and enthusiasm. People hurt us; we are disappointed and feel disillusioned; we don't have the resources to continue. Any number of things can cause us to stop. We may stop permanently, or we may just get distracted and eventually pick up the ball and continue running. In football, when a player is going for the goal line and is stopped by the other team, that player's team has to start again from the spot where they were stopped. When that happens, they may try a whole different strategy for how to advance the ball toward the goal.

If you are reading this and find yourself in a stopped position or distracted, with one thing or another, from the touchdown of your personal prophetic words, consider picking up the ball and continue running. These words Paul wrote to Timothy apply to you, too:

> *For this reason I remind you to fan into flame the gift of God, which is in you through the laying on of my hands. For the Spirit God gave us does not make us timid, but gives us power, love and self-discipline* (2 Timothy 1:6–7).

Here again we see how easily we can become apathetic and distracted from our course. We must be ever diligent to stir up the gift given to us, to fan the flame of the gift of God. Prophecy has a tendency to settle, and it is our responsibility to stir it up! It is not God's job but ours.

It is vitally important for us to grab hold of this truth and change our minds, if necessary, regarding our responsibility to our personal prophetic words. We must cooperate with God in order for the words to be fulfilled. God will not bring them to pass all by Himself. Once God has spoken a prophetic word to us, we have a responsibility to work *with Him* toward the fulfillment of that word. Of course, He does not want us to go off on our own and strive to bring it to pass on our own strength, but we do have a part to play.

First Timothy 1 contains helpful guidelines for how to respond to prophecies we receive:

> *Timothy, my son, I am giving you this command in keeping with the prophecies once made about you, so that by recalling them you may fight the battle well, holding on to faith and a good conscience, which some have rejected and so have suffered shipwreck with regard to the faith* (1 Timothy 1:18–19).

Here Paul commanded Timothy to fight a good warfare with the prophecies spoken over him. God will sometimes speak to us through a prophetic word and give us insight into a situation. Then He expects us to pray and intercede and war with that word until it comes to pass. Instead of walking around with the assumption that since God spoke it He will just make it happen, we need to press in by faith and call forth prophetic realities that do not yet exist in the natural as though they already did (see Rom. 4:17). This is warring with the prophetic.

Prophecy always speaks to our potential. It is not unconditional, meaning God does not guarantee our personal words will come to pass. We must actively participate, working along with God to bring the words to pass. Personal prophecy is not equal to the written Word of God, which is the only thing that will be completely and perfectly fulfilled whether we are involved or not. Because of this, it is important for us to get involved with our prophetic words and learn how to interact with God to help bring them to pass.

Testing the Word

Of course, as we've stated before, the first step after receiving a prophetic word is to test it to see whether it is from God. Following are eight steps that will help you put the prophetic words you receive to the test.

1. Write out the prophecy word-for-word.

This is a time-consuming task, but it is well worth it. We can easily miss words and thoughts when we only listen to the recording, but when we actually have the word in black and white on paper, it is much simpler to study it carefully. A couple Scripture passages show us how Old Testament prophets handled words they received. In Daniel 7:1 we read, *"Daniel had a dream, and visions passed through his mind as he was lying in bed. He wrote down the substance of his dream."* Also, Habakkuk was instructed, *"Write down the revelation and make it plain on tablets so that a herald may run with it"* (Hab. 2:2). I understand this verse to say that if the message is written out clearly, the person reading it will be able to take action on what it says. How can we run if we don't understand the message?

Please take the time to write out your personal prophetic words, as well as dreams and visions. They should all be tested and acted on in the same way. If we treat what God is saying to us as important (by writing it down), He will continue to speak to us.

2. Put the prophetic message to the Scripture test.

As we read previously, Paul commanded us, *"Do not quench the Spirit. Do not treat prophecies with contempt but test them all; hold on to what is good"* (1 Thess. 5:19–21). Here is a simple and practical way to test whether a prophetic word honors God and upholds Scriptures.

Once you have written out your prophetic words exactly and in totality, begin to pray about them and ask the Lord to bring portions of Scripture to your mind that may go along with or back up parts of the prophecy. Scripture may be quoted within the context of the prophecy, or it may contain scriptural principles. We like to find as many verses as possible to consider. For instance, if the Lord says He is going to enlarge your sphere of influence, you might think of Isaiah 54:2, which says, *"Enlarge the place of your tent, stretch your tent curtains wide...,"* or Psalm 18:36, which says, *"You provide a broad path for my feet, so that my ankles do not give way."*

You may automatically think of certain verses, but it may also be necessary to use your handy concordance and look up key words and ideas. You can also use websites like biblegateway.com or other computer software. It is important to find the scriptural basis for the prophecy. When you do, often the verses will broaden your understanding of what God is saying to you.

3. Consider whether your spirit bears witness to the word with peace.

Romans 8:16 tells us, *"The Spirit himself testifies with our spirit..."* This is referring to our identity as children of God, but it is a principle that applies to other areas as well. If we feel uncomfortable about something, we need to ask ourselves why. Do we need to change our minds about something because we now have more information on the subject, or is the Spirit causing us to feel uneasy because what is going on is not really from Him? Only you, as the individual, can answer that, and I would encourage you to not be too hasty in your decision. Take sufficient time to consider the word that has been spoken and to pray about it. God has put within you the ability to discern whether or not it is from Him:

> *You have an anointing from the Holy One, and all of you know the truth....The anointing you received from him remains in you...[and] teaches you about all things...* (1 John 2:20, 27).

This statement from John that we *"know the truth"* should encourage us to take seriously the peace (or lack of peace) we feel in our spirits. If we are willing to listen, He will help us understand.

Colossians 3:15 tells us, *"Let the peace of Christ rule in your hearts..."* Peace should be the ruler in our hearts. It should be the atmosphere we live in. If it is, when something enters and disturbs that peace, we will notice it and be able to take it seriously. For a follower of Christ, anything that causes a lack of peace is a foreign object, like a splinter is to our fingers. It disturbs us until we rid ourselves of it. Never ignore that gnawing feeling you have inside, even if you may not be able to explain it. Most likely the Holy Spirit is warning you or trying to protect you from harm in some way.

4. *Divide the prophetic word into three sections.*

It is vitally important to determine what is God's part and what is our part, because He is not going to do our part, and we are definitely not able to do His part. We can save ourselves a lot of heartache if we learn this principle early. Too many of us spend too much time trying to bring something to pass when He is simply asking us to cooperate with Him. For this reason, this simple exercise involving dividing the prophetic word into three sections is extremely helpful.

You can do this several different ways. You may want to take three sheets of paper and write on the top of one, *God's Part*; on the top of the second, *My Part*; and on the top of the third, *Specifics*. Or you may want to use three different colored highlighters, with each color representing one of these three categories. Once you have chosen how to proceed, begin to write out or mark the portions of the prophetic word in which God says He is going to do something—with no conditions attached. That is what we call *God's Part*.

Next, write out or mark those portions in which He says specifically what He expects you to do, actions He directs you to take, and so forth. This may be absolutely direct, or it may be spoken as a condition. A condition may sound like: "I have given you a gift of prophecy, and I want you to begin to step out and look for those around you who need encouragement. Begin to enter into this gift that I have placed in your life." Within this hypothetical prophecy are three steps that are the responsibility of the person receiving it:

1. Begin to step out.
2. Look for those around you.
3. Begin to enter in.

Numbers 1 and 3 are almost exactly the same thing. They are an exhortation to take action. Number 2 is an example of how to begin to take the action—look for those around you. These are actions God is not going to do for the person. Instead, He expects the person to do them in obedience to the word. Therefore, they belong under *My Part*.

Finally, write out or mark those portions referring to anything specific He may have mentioned—things like certain gifts, talents, abilities, or callings. In our hypothetical prophecy above, He mentions a gift of prophecy. This page or marker may not have very many things; in some cases, it may have none at all. But if there are any, it is helpful to know what gifts He says you have or should be functioning in. You can then begin to look up Scriptures to learn about these gifts. You may want to get some books on the subject. And you may even want to talk with others who already function in those gifts. Best of all is if you are able to find a way to be involved and grow in the use of the gifts.

If He mentions a *Specific*—such as healing, prophecy, teaching, or missions—we recommend first saying *amen* to Him and embracing the word He has spoken to you (even if you feel unfitted for the word, which usually is the case). Then begin to read and study all you can about that specific area. If your church has something already in place, where you can volunteer and get involved in the specific area and begin to practice your gift, that is a very good next step. As you grow, you should just keep taking opportunities that you become aware of along the lines of that *Specific*. As you do, you will find yourself gaining confidence and understanding. More and more doors will begin to open for you. And as you choose to step through them, you will find that you have become a part of the fulfillment of your own prophetic word.

Please don't expect to become a healing evangelist who is holding huge crusades overnight if you have never even dared to lay your hands on a sick person and pray for healing. Almost always God will begin a process that we can take part in, and over a period of time, we will find that we have grown into the person He talked about in the prophecy.

When He speaks to us prophetically, we are usually not anywhere near being the person He calls us in the prophecy. He sees us differently than we see ourselves, and He sees us according to our destiny instead of where we really are. He sees us as the mature, finished product He knows He can make us into, if we will just let Him have His way in our lives. Thus, He speaks to our potential, and then He helps us grow into it.

5. Consider seeking counsel.

Proverbs tells us of the connection between seeking counsel and making a wise decision. *"For lack of guidance a nation falls, but victory is won through many advisers"* (Prov. 11:14; see Prov. 15:22; 24:6). Of course, it is important to find counselors who believe prophecy is a gift for today. And it is helpful to seek out those who are knowledgeable of the written Word as well. What you don't want to do is look for someone you know will automatically side with you and your viewpoint. This will not be helpful in the long-run. You want someone who will be willing to challenge you if you're seeing it wrongly.

6. You must already be walking in all the Scripture you understand.

God uses people who are less than perfect, but if people are willfully living contrary to the Word of God, it will greatly hinder them from going forward, no matter what prophetic words they have received.

7. Remember that prophecy is only one part of guidance.

Prophecy is only one part of guidance and the process by which you determine your direction in life. We have known too many people through the years who based their decisions solely on a word of prophecy. Some sold their homes, quit their jobs, and moved across the country strictly on a word of prophecy. They did not test it, seek counsel, give time, or wait for other things to line up as a confirmation. They just ran off—some to their own detriment! When this happens, the good name of prophecy (and even God) gets a bad rap, and disappointment and unbelief set in. All these hardships can be avoided if we keep prophecy in its rightful place—as just one avenue of guidance.

8. Give God time.

Part of life in the Spirit is learning to hold the things we hear and see in our hearts and give God time to work them out! (See Gen. 37:11; Dan. 7:28; Luke 2:51.) We should not be in a hurry, even though the prophecy may be very exciting. God knows the perfect timing, and He knows what we need before we will be ready for the fulfillment of the word. When God gave Joseph dreams about his destiny, Joseph was not yet the person who could step into the responsibility God was calling Him to, and Egypt did not yet need what he had to give. But years later, when the need arose in Egypt, Joseph was finally ready to step into his position and fulfill the words given to him. Give God the time necessary to make you into the person He needs you to be in order to meet the needs He's calling you to.

nine

Fencing Out Deception

Many people avoid involvement with the prophetic and other supernatural gifts of the Spirit because they are concerned about being deceived. When prophecy is mentioned, they immediately begin talking about the New Age movement, psychics, witches, mediums, and the like. Thankfully, God has put several safeguards—or fences—in place to help prevent His children from falling into deception and wandering astray. (For more information about counterfeits versus the authentic gifts of God, see *New Age Masquerade* by Jonathan Welton)

Fence 1: The Definitive Test

The definitive test examines whose name the prophecy is being given in. This is outlined in First Corinthians 12:3, where the apostle Paul writes:

> *Therefore I want you to know that no one who is speaking by the Spirit of God says, "Jesus be cursed," and no one can say, "Jesus is Lord," except by the Holy Spirit.*

Old Testament prophets delivered messages from God by saying, "Thus says the Lord"—which served to distinguish God's voice from the voices of the many other gods worshipped by the people of that day.

The true prophets wanted to make sure the people understood *who* was speaking to them. In the same way, kings throughout history have put their names on proclamations as proof the message truly came from them and would be backed up by them. Now, when we prophesy, people generally understand we are speaking for God, and we do not need to affix the name of God to a prophetic message to try to give it more authority. However, if the prophecy is given in the name of someone other than the God of the Scriptures, it is a false message and should be ignored.

This is how we know the spirit of truth and the spirit of error. The apostle John also mentions this test in his first epistle:

> *Dear friends, do not believe every spirit, but test the spirits to see whether they are from God, because many false prophets have gone out into the world. This is how you can recognize the Spirit of God: Every spirit that acknowledges that Jesus Christ has come in the flesh is from God, but every spirit that does not acknowledge Jesus is not from God. This is the spirit of the antichrist, which you have heard is coming and even now is already in the world* (1 John 4:1–3).

In other words, any person who does not acknowledge the divinity of Jesus and does not seek to glorify God (but rather self) is not speaking on God's behalf and is a false prophet. We should not ever listen to or consider words given by such a person. If a word is given in the name of the speaker (giving directions or commands to follow the speaker), we need to reject that word. If the word is given in the name of any other god or gods, we must automatically reject the word. If it mentions anyone or anything else other than Jesus Christ the Lord as a supreme being, it is false and should be discarded immediately! It is not from God if it does not honor Jesus Christ as God.

All prophecies must pass this particular test before they should be considered further. If they do not pass this test, they are automatically rejected. Often we will not need this test because we will know the person speaking believes Jesus Christ is God's Son. However, it is good to be mindful of it, as several cults have had their beginnings in exactly this sort of deception. The prophetic words and messengers were not tested, found false, and disregarded. Rather, they were pursued and studied way beyond the parameters of the first fence and, therefore, led to deception.

Fence 2: The Gift of Discerning of Spirits

In Chapter 5, we discussed the gift of discerning of spirits, which is highlighted in First Corinthians 12:10 among the spiritual gifts given to the body of Christ. This gift is specifically designed as a protective fence for the body of Christ. Through it, God the Father helps us walk with Him and not wander from the sheep pen. This gift is especially important within the Church, because it can help us detect whether something is of the Holy Spirit, the human spirit, the angelic, or an evil spirit. Some situations will warrant us testing what is going on in order to determine the source of the prophecy. Obviously, knowing what spirit is at work among us is extremely important to the health of the body of Christ.

If we don't know the source, how can we know how to appropriately respond? If the Holy Spirit is the source, we need to get involved with His work. But what if a person's human spirit is the source? Certainly we don't want to simply receive such prophecies as the word of God. That could lead to a complete derailing of God's purposes for that group of people. Instead, with the help of the gift of discerning of spirits, we can discern when people are prophesying from their own perceptions. If these people are afraid and exuding fear, we must find out why and lead them toward freedom. If they are insecure and lack confidence, this can manifest in one of two ways. They may be timid, retiring, and shy, or they may come across as very confident, almost to the point of seeming proud. They may be controlling and manipulative—causing others to feel about an inch tall.

One way the gift of discernment operates is through unusual emotions when we are around a certain person. In other words, if you leave a person's presence feeling like you are "so insecure" (when you normally do not struggle with insecurity), what has happened is you have discerned the other person's human spirit. Similarly, if you find yourself thinking or feeling lustful thoughts (that you normally do not struggle with) whenever you are around a certain person, it's a good sign these thoughts and feelings are not coming from within you. Instead, you may be discerning the other person's human spirit or even an evil spirit at work in that person. (When people open their human spirits to pride, lust, fear, and so forth, they open the door to allow evil spirits to begin to work in and through them.)

In these examples we see that the gift of discerning of spirits, when not regularly cultivated and matured, can be confusing and easy to overlook. When people don't know what to do with something, they will often discard it. Too often this supernatural gift is disregarded as "a sixth sense" or women's intuition. People who have a strong gift of discernment are sometimes accused of being too sensitive or spooky. They often feel ignored and sometimes even rejected. Because of a lack of understanding, many people who have this gift are not taught how to properly use it, and as a result, the body of Christ suffers from a lack of discernment. Once this subject is taught on, those same people will often begin to feel free to share from their experiences, and they will feel affirmed. They may have thought they were crazy or, at the very least, a bit strange; some even say they thought they were losing their minds! Most likely they were questioning their experiences because they didn't have a grid for understanding them. People can go on like this for years, holding it inside because they don't have anyone they feel safe talking to. This is sad and very unfortunate because we need this gift functioning in our churches and fellowship groups. But leaders can only lead people where they themselves have been or are willing to go.

In all this we see how incredibly important the gift of discernment is as a fence protecting the body of Christ from deception. We don't want to unknowingly partner with the evil realm while believing we are following the Holy Spirit. Neither do we want to think everything is fine when, in reality, we should be talking with the person and possibly casting out an evil spirit. The Bible tells us some people come into the body of believers as wolves in sheep's clothing, but without the gift of discernment, they can be difficult to spot until a lot of damage has been done (see Matt. 7:15). Other people simply need to be taught how to deal with their own human spirits and to discern when their own spirits are not cooperating well with the Holy Spirit. Building up this fence for the body of Christ will bring increased safety for the use of spiritual gifts and the supernatural.

Fence 3: General Spiritual Discernment

Not only does the body of Christ have certain members who possess the gift of discernment of spirits, but all believers also have a general ability to discern spiritually. When believers come together, they corporately experience increased discernment regarding what is taking place in the spiritual realm. Hebrews 5:14 says, *"Solid food is for the mature, who by constant use have trained themselves to distinguish good from evil."* From this verse we see it is possible to grow in discernment by using it, much like one becomes stronger through physical exercise. As leaders make room for this discernment in corporate gatherings, without being too quick to dismiss what is being shared, people will have an opportunity to mature in discernment, and the body will benefit from a greater spiritual awareness.

The reason so many leaders hesitate to allow room for discernment is because many believers respond immaturely to what they discern due to a lack of training. Here's the key: When we become aware of something negative in the spirit realm, we need to handle it with restoration as our top priority. It's too easy for judgment and condemnation to play a part in discernment. But the Holy Spirit reveals such things so something good can take place. He does not want to embarrass or destroy someone or some place; He wants restoration, reconciliation, and encouragement to be the end product of our discernment.

This is why such verses as First Corinthians 14:29—*"Two or three prophets should speak, and the others should weigh carefully what is said"*—and First Thessalonians 5:21—*"Test them all [prophecies]; hold on to what is good"*—are so important. We need to learn to work together corporately, making room for one another and the sensitivities the Lord has placed in each other. We need all the members of the body working together in harmony—even those we don't understand as well as others.

Fence 4: Diligent Study of All the Scriptures

As we've already mentioned, God has given us the Scriptures as a standard to help us discern truth. This means we will have a hard time discerning the validity of prophetic words if we do not regularly read, study, and hide the Scriptures in our hearts. The Bible determines what is sound doctrine, and the only way we can know sound doctrine is by reading and studying it (see Titus 2:1, 7–8). Paul described the importance of this in his letter to Titus:

> *He must hold firmly to the trustworthy message as it has been taught, so that he can encourage others by sound doctrine and refute those who oppose it* (Titus 1:9).

To properly test a prophetic word against Scripture, we need to use the whole counsel of Scripture (both Old and New Testaments)—carefully comparing text with text and not taking verses out of context to make them fit our own desires. When we learn to rightly divide the Word of God (see 2 Tim. 2:15) and have it rooted in our hearts, as the anchor we can pull on when judging prophecy, we will experience the full benefits and safety of the fence of God's Word to protect the body of Christ from deception.

Fence 5: The Standard of Edification, Exhortation, and Comfort

In First Corinthians 14:3, we have this standard for prophecy: *"But the one who prophesies speaks to people for their strengthening, encouraging and comfort"* (1 Cor. 14:3). The New King James Version uses the words *"edification and exhortation and comfort."* Let's look at these three standards more closely.

Edify is defined as: "to instruct and improve especially in moral and religious knowledge, to build, establish, uplift, enlighten, inform." *Encourage* is often used interchangeably with *edify*. *Encouragement* is defined as: "to inspire with courage, spirit, hope, to spur on, to stimulate, to give help." En-courage-ment is the act of putting courage into someone. When the Lord says He sees you a certain way, He is attempting to put courage into you. When He says you can do a certain thing, He is attempting to put courage into you. When He says, "Fear not," "Have courage," or, "Step out," He is trying to put courage into you.

The story of Gideon gives us a good example of the power of edification (see Judg. 6–7). Gideon was a man of Israel who was so afraid of the Midianites (their attacking enemies) that he was hiding in a very large wine press. His vision was only as big as being able to thresh out enough wheat for himself and his family without being seen or caught by their enemies. Into this scenario, the Angel of the Lord appears and calls Gideon *"you mighty man of valor"* (Judg. 6:12). Such a name is absolutely contradictory to the situation and to how Gideon thought of himself. No one saw him as a mighty man of valor—except God. God knew what Gideon was capable of, so He spoke His edifying and encouraging word to Gideon, calling him to elevate himself to God's vision of him. Through his commendation of Gideon as a mighty man of valor, God changed Gideon's viewpoint, and his actions followed accordingly. God knew that changing how Gideon saw himself would affect his actions and cause him to live up to his new identity. Israel needed a mighty man of valor, so God called out Gideon and told him who he really was and what he could really do, and as a result, Gideon overcame the Midianites by the power of God.

This is how prophecy works. It is supposed to bring God's perspective and intentions into a desperate situation in order to bring change. It is meant to bring love, peace, joy, freedom, and confidence—to correct any lack or error in our perspective of ourselves and our calling. If God can use someone to speak His thoughts and desires; if He can get someone else to hear, believe, and act on what He's saying; He can bring victory into otherwise gloomy situations.

Exhort is defined as: "to urge strongly; to give warnings or advice; to make urgent appeals." *Exhortation* carries the connotation of urging or stimulating someone to action. God knows this life has a way of lulling us to sleep and entangling our feet. Those who want to be judgmental and harsh tend to assume *exhort* means just saying what they have to say, laying the truth out there, and giving someone else a good talking-to! But that approach usually leaves the hearer feeling desperate and rejected. They are left with no hope. This is definitely not God's intention for prophetic exhortation. When He speaks to us directly or through His people, it is always for the purpose of waking us up, stirring us to action, and setting us free to fulfill His will for our lives. As Hebrews 10:24–25 says:

> *And let us consider how we may spur one another on toward love and good deeds, not giving up meeting together, as some are in the habit of doing, but encouraging one another—and all the more as you see the Day approaching.*

This verse, unfortunately, is usually used to tell people they are required to attend a church regularly. The original readers were the Hebrew Christians who were being tested horribly for their faith in Christ. Life was so difficult for them that many were drawing back and no longer gathering together for fear of being found. They had been suffering the loss of their earthly goods (see Heb 10:34). This was the relevance of this verse to those early Christians to whom the letter was written. Through it, they were being encouraged to continued gathering and fellowshipping together in order to build one another up and continue on in the face of persecution. It exhorted them to continue in the kind of fellowship with other believers where exhortation, open sharing, stirring each other up to take action on the will of God, and comfort for life's struggles would take place. The point is, exhortation is intended to inspire and encourage, not to cut others down.

Comfort is defined as: "consolation in the time of trouble or worry." It is relief or encouragement; a contented well-being; a satisfying or enjoyable experience (the comfort of a good meal after hard work); to strengthen greatly; to give strength and hope to; to ease grief and trouble. *Comfort* is anything that brings strength, hope, sympathy, ease, or satisfaction into our lives. In John 14:16, the Holy Spirit is called the Comforter, showing us that comfort is a big part of how God relates to His people. Isaiah 40:1–2 shows God's heart, even in the Old Testament, to comfort His people: *"'Comfort, yes, comfort My people!' says your God. 'Speak comfort to Jerusalem…'"*

In these three standards—edification, exhortation, and comfort—we find our final fence with which we can test the accuracy of prophetic words and protect the body of believers from deception. No matter how accurate a word may seem, if it does not reflect these three standards, it does not reflect the heart of God and has the potential to lead people into deception.

Thankfully, God did not simply give us the supernatural gifts of the Spirit with no instruction for how to protect against error and deception. No, His love for us and His desire for us to experience the fullness of life aligned with His truth caused Him to give us fences that enable us to determine whether or not a prophecy or supernatural experience is from Him.

ten

Balaam and the False Prophets

People who fear the potential of deception related to prophecy often bring up the subject of false prophets. Certainly, it is an important issue to address. False prophets do exist. However, a false prophet is not simply someone who gets a prophecy wrong. False prophecy and mistaken prophecy are not the same. A false prophet is someone who is intentionally misleading people. *What makes a prophet or a prophecy false or true is the motivation behind the words.* In order to understand what a false prophet looks like, first let's look at the much more common instance of mistaken or misdirected prophecy.

Mistaken or Misdirected Words

We all need to be aware that we can slip into prophesying out of our own thoughts and desires and calling them the word of the Lord. Sometimes, when we stretch out too far beyond our faith level, we may enter into presumption. This does not make us false prophets, and it is not an indication that we should stop prophesying, either. It just shows we are in the process of learning, and we need to grow some more. People are not false just because they make a mistake. We may all miss things when we are learning and practicing. We may think we're hearing God's voice, but we really are hearing a mixture. This is part of learning to hear God's voice. Even the prophets in the Old Testament sometimes got words wrong because they misheard God or prophesied from their own desires. Consider the prophet Nathan:

> *Nathan replied to David, "Whatever you have in mind, do it, for God is with you." But that night the word of God came to Nathan, saying: "Go and tell my servant David, 'This is what the LORD says: You are not the one to build me a house to dwell in'"* (1 Chronicles 17:2).

Nathan's initial response to David's desire to build the temple came out of his own emotions and love for David, who was his friend. He didn't think before he spoke. He wanted so much for David to be blessed that he spoke out of his own desire—not the word of the Lord. It is so easy to fall into this when we are with others. They may be sharing some of their thoughts with us, and if we're not careful, we quickly say something like, "Go for it, Helen! It's a great idea!" If we are people who are attempting to speak in connection with the Spirit (and perhaps we even have reputations and positions regarding this), it is very important to guard what we say to others. They may take it very seriously and may even take action on what we say. They may take our comments as prophecy when, in reality, we were just speaking flippantly.

When the word of God came to Nathan that night, it was different from what Nathan had told David. Nathan's heart was full of love toward David, but he didn't see things the way God saw them. He had to go back to David the next morning and correct his message. Nathan never intended to deceive or lead David astray from God. He simply slipped out of speaking for the Lord and crossed over into his own friendly emotions. This is so easy to do, but if we want to be used by the Spirit in prophecy, we need to be very careful about how we allow ourselves to speak. We may want something to happen so badly that we begin to prophesy it. This is a way of controlling and manipulating situations to make them go the way we think they should go. Some prophets in the Old Testament did this very thing. As Ezekiel 13:2 says, *"...Say to those who prophesy out of their own imagination: 'Hear the word of the LORD.'"* They were putting their own thoughts and desires into prophetic words and calling them the "word of the Lord."

Another example of a true prophet delivering a prophecy that contained an error is found in the New Testament, in the prophet Agabus, who prophesied about Paul's arrest:

> *After we had been there a number of days, a prophet named Agabus came down from Judea. Coming over to us, he took Paul's belt, tied his own hands and feet with it and said, "The Holy Spirit says, 'In this way the Jewish leaders in Jerusalem will bind the owner of this belt and will hand him over to the Gentiles'"* (Acts 21:10–11).

Here Agabus is called a prophet, and that is not disputed anywhere else in the New Testament. From this we can safely assume he was, in fact, a legitimate prophet. In his prophecy, Agabus uses Paul's own belt as a prop, acting out a prophetic message indicating that Paul will be delivered into the hands of the Gentiles. The problem is, when the time came, it didn't happen quite as Agabus said. The Jews planned and attempted to kill Paul, but the Romans actually saved Paul from the Jew's plot against his life. Paul then spent many years as a Roman prisoner until he was eventually killed in Rome. A minor detail was incorrect, yet this fact did not cause Agabus to be named a false prophet. Clearly, the falseness of a prophet is not determined by the accuracy of the prophecy.

Genuine False Prophets

What does determine falseness, then? We find our answer in another New Testament character, Simon the sorcerer. Simon was awestruck by the disciples' power and the signs they performed, and he offered to pay them money to purchase the ability to lay hands on people and impart the Holy Spirit (see Acts 8:18–24). It's not clear whether he was motivated by the prestige or the money he could make through this ability. What is clear is that his motive was wrong. He had the makings of a false prophet within him, because falseness is not determined by inaccuracy of the word but by wrong motives in the heart.

This is why we must be very careful not to use our spiritual gifts for our own selfish ambitions and desires. We also must be very careful not to use prophecy to manipulate others into doing what we think they should do. Manipulation and control under the guise of prophecy are a form of witchcraft. We will always do our best when we practice our gifts in connection with a God-given authority—such as a pastor, elder, teacher, or prophet with whom we have on-going relationship. In this relationship, we must be open and willing to be corrected. And when we give a prophetic word, we should always welcome others to test our words and give feedback, recognizing that we all need to learn and grow in the use of our gifts.

False prophets often teach false doctrines. We see this in Jesus' concern for what would happen to the early Church after He was gone. He wanted His disciples to understand how to tell the false from the true; He knew the damage the false could bring to His people (see Matt. 24:24; Mark 13:22; Luke 6:26). He warned His disciples:

> *Watch out for false prophets. They come to you in sheep's clothing, but inwardly they are ferocious wolves. By their fruit you will recognize them. Do people pick grapes from thornbushes, or figs from thistles? Likewise, every good tree bears good fruit, but a bad tree bears bad fruit. A good tree cannot bear bad fruit, and a bad tree cannot bear good fruit. Every tree that does not bear good fruit is cut down and thrown into the fire. Thus, by their fruit you will recognize them* (Matthew 7:15–20).

Here again we see that the falseness is not always easily recognizable to our natural discernment. It is a heart issue. But the fruit tells us the truth. In Paul's first letter to Timothy, he also warned his spiritual son to watch out for false prophets, including those who *"follow deceiving spirits and things taught by demons"* (1 Tim. 4:1). These heretical teachings will come through *"hypocritical liars, whose consciences have been seared as with a hot iron"* (1 Tim. 4:2). The word translated *seared* here means "to become callous or insensitive." Such individuals no longer care about the ramifications of their actions, and they are not motivated by God's heart for people but for their own personal gain. Paul goes on to say that these false prophets will forbid people from marrying, command people to abstain from certain foods, and speak lies in hypocrisy (see 1 Tim. 4:2-3). In other words, they would exercise control and manipulation in people's lives by legislating personal matters, such as marriage and diet choices.

The necessary responses to these false teachings are found in First Timothy 4:4-7:

> *For everything God created is good, and nothing is to be rejected if it is received with thanksgiving, because it is consecrated by the word of God and prayer. If you point these things out to the brothers and sisters, you will be a good minister of Christ Jesus, nourished on the truths of the faith and of the good teaching that you have followed. Have nothing to do with godless myths and old wives' tales; rather, train yourself to be godly.*

In other words, the response to false prophecy and false teaching is to hold fast to orthodox Christian doctrine according to the Word of God. Hebrews 13:8-9 also addresses this, saying, *"Jesus Christ is the same yesterday and today and forever. Do not be carried away by all kinds of strange teachings. It is good for our hearts to be strengthened by grace...."* We can count on the steadfastness of Christ. He is the same *always* and *for all time*, and anything that deviates from what we read of Him in the New Testament must be categorized as false doctrine. Of course, some may mistakenly teach false doctrines because of a lack of understanding and information. This does not make a person a false teacher. But teachers who purposely choose to deviate from the sound doctrine of the Scriptures may be categorized as false teachers. Our standard must always be formed by looking at *what* Jesus did and *how* He did it. His standard is forever true, throughout all eternity.

Recognizing False Prophets

False prophets still exist today, as they have since the days of the early Church. They have no serious love or concern for people but are seeking to lead people away from God and after themselves through their teachings and prophecies. Following are three primary characteristics of all false prophets.

1. False prophets seek to turn people away from the truth.

In Acts 13, Paul encountered a sorcerer named Elymas who was intentionally opposing Paul's ministry and trying to turn the proconsul *away* from the faith. This was not accidental but very purposeful and rooted in a heart-opposition to the things of God. In response, Paul rebuked Elymas as a child of the devil, full of deceit and trickery, who perverted the right ways of the Lord. And he caused Elymas to become blind as a sign of God's power (see Acts 13:6–12). In this instance, Elymas was not claiming to be a Christian, but he was claiming to speak for God and, thereby, turning people away from the true faith. Many false prophets claim to be Christians in order to lead Christians away from God. Paul mentioned false apostles who masqueraded as servants of righteousness while covertly teaching false doctrines:

> *And I will keep on doing what I am doing in order to cut the ground from under those who want an opportunity to be considered equal with us in the things they boast about. For such people are false apostles, deceitful workers, masquerading as apostles of Christ. And no wonder, for Satan himself masquerades as an angel of light. It is not surprising,*

then, if his servants also masquerade as servants of righteousness. Their end will be what their actions deserve (2 Corinthians 11:12–15).

The reality of false prophets shows the importance of testing every doctrine against the Word of God. When we do that, we will not be led away from the truth.

2. False prophets seek to draw people to follow after themselves.

When false prophets lead people away from the truth, they do it in order to convince people to follow them. Paul warned the early Church about this reality, saying:

> *Keep watch over yourselves and all the flock of which the Holy Spirit has made you overseers. Be shepherds of the church of God, which he bought with his own blood. I know that after I leave, savage wolves will come in among you and will not spare the flock. Even from your own number men will arise and distort the truth in order to draw away disciples after them* (Acts 20:28–30).

Here we clearly see that false prophets can arise from within the Church and seek to draw people after themselves. When Christian are drawn to follow a human leader in an unhealthy and extreme manner, instead of following Christ as the leader of us all, churches and groups can quickly become toxic and even cultish.

3. False prophets have no real love or concern for people.

The apostle Peter mentioned the lack of true love false prophets have for people. Though they may appear to care about people, that caring comes with an agenda to control.

> *But there were also false prophets among the people, just as there will be false teachers among you. They will secretly introduce destructive heresies, even denying the sovereign Lord*

> *who bought them—bringing swift destruction on themselves. Many will follow their depraved conduct and will bring the way of truth into disrepute. In their greed these teachers will exploit you with fabricated stories. Their condemnation has long been hanging over them, and their destruction has not been sleeping* (2 Peter 2:1–3).

False prophets are willing to exploit people to get what they want, and they use prophecy to do it. True prophets only prophesy out of a love for people rooted in the Father's heart. A true prophet will work hard to bring people into their true identity in Christ and all He has obtained for them in the New Covenant. The prophet will rejoice to see people beginning to understand who they are in Christ and His destiny for their lives—to see them beginning to walk in freedom and truth. The true prophet wants people to be blessed and set free to enter into all the Kingdom provisions secured in Christ's suffering, death, and resurrection. True prophets are motivated to empower people to freely follow God more fully, not to gather people around themselves.

Jim Jones (1931-1978) is a modern example of a false prophet. He began as a minister of the gospel but turned away from the truth and began to teach heresy, all the while gathering followers to himself. He became like their god, and in the end, he orchestrated a mass suicide, convincing over nine hundred men, women, and children to drink poisoned juice in the jungle of Guyana—including some who did not want to die. This was the greatest single loss of American civilian life in a deliberate act until the attack on the World Trade Center on September 11, 2001.

We have seen up-close how a false prophet operates. Years ago, we were part of a church whose pastor was an excellent Bible teacher with a wonderful reputation. We loved him dearly, as did our children and so many of our friends and acquaintances. However, over time he began to teach strange things that were not biblical. Some were not able to distinguish the difference between truth and error, even those who had attended seminary and Bible schools. Looking back, we compare this to a frog being boiled alive in hot water. A frog is a cold-blooded creature, and if it is thrown directly into hot, boiling water, it will instinctively jump right back out because of the temperature difference. But if the frog is put into cold water and over time the water is heated to boiling point, the frog will not notice the change, because its body temperature will adjust upward along with the water. Therefore, it will stay right there and be boiled alive.

This is exactly what seemed to happen in this particular church. The pastor had so ingratiated himself with the people and their families that we all felt we could relax and trust him. We never thought anything bad could happen while he was the pastor. But as the years passed, some of us began to notice little bits of error sneaking into the teaching. We would try to reconcile what we were hearing with what we thought we knew of the pastor, and we would dismiss it by saying things such as, "Oh, he must mean this...." Eventually, the errors began to be more and more blatant, and we began to say to ourselves, "Now wait a minute! This man is an excellent orator and Bible teacher. If he meant a certain thing, he would say it clearly." Then we began to consider what outsiders would hear if they listened to his teaching. The outsiders would not have the same "love and respect filter" we all had and through which we sifted his teachings. As we considered this, we realized this man meant exactly what he was saying. He knew what he was teaching and where he intended to take as many followers as possible. We began listening to his teachings as if we were strangers with no "love filter" and making note of what we were hearing. We tried talking with him directly about these things several times, but we received no real answers from him.

During the time when we were still parishioners, the pastor began holding special meetings during the weekdays that certain people would attend in order to understand more fully his "new revelation." Week after week, he would indoctrinate and methodically brainwash these followers. One lady, who was a dear friend of mine, regularly attended the teaching sessions. As she "changed her mind" and imbibed the "new revelation," she told me she experienced physical reactions to the teachings. She mentioned having to leave the room and vomit sometimes because she felt so sick. But even then, she continued attending and imbibing, and eventually she could attend without reactions. She had become a follower. And little by little, they began to let go of the cardinal doctrines of the faith, as taught in the Scriptures, and they increasingly embraced the falsehoods they were being taught so carefully.

Our experience at that church shows why it is so important to search the Scriptures. We must regularly search the Bible and test what we are hearing and seeing to be sure we are being led more and more into love with Christ Jesus of the Bible and farther away from sin and idolatry. Following after a person as though that person is a god, as our friends at our former church did, is in fact idolatry. If someone is leading us away from the truth that is in Christ Jesus of the Bible and gathering us to follow after him or herself, we have to conclude that this person is a false prophet and teacher. And we should pull back from listening to or heeding any of the words this person gives. This is a very serious matter, and it can have very disastrous results in our lives. We cannot underestimate the importance of correct doctrine. I don't mean we all need to study theology, but I do mean we all need to know the basic and essential doctrines of the Christian faith—and why they are true from Scripture. As we discussed at the beginning of this book, Scripture is our anchor that protects us from deception and false teaching.

The Test of a False Prophet

We've talked about what sets false prophets apart from mistaken prophets, and we've looked at the three main characteristics of false prophets. Now let's consider some questions we can ask when discerning whether a person is a false prophet. These questions will equip us to recognize error and avoid being slowly boiled by heretical teachings like a frog in a pot of water.

Where are they leading us?

This is the most important question to ask in determining whether or not people are false prophets. In the Old Testament, Moses told the Israelites:

> *If a prophet, or one who foretells by dreams, appears among you and announces to you a sign or wonder, and if the sign or wonder spoken of takes place, and the prophet says, "Let us follow other gods" (gods you have not known) "and let us worship them," you must not listen to the words of that prophet or dreamer. The LORD your God is testing you to find out whether you love him with all your heart and with all your soul. It is the LORD your God you must follow, and him you must revere. Keep his commands and obey him; serve him and hold fast to him* (Deuteronomy 13:1–4).

Here we see that it may be possible for a false prophet to perform signs or wonders and to give accurate prophecies. These manifestations of the supernatural are no proof that the person's power comes from God. Certainly, if someone claiming to be a prophet regularly gives prophecies that are proven wrong, that is a sign we should not listen to that person; however, manifestations of power and accurate prophetic words cannot be the *only* test we give to determine a false prophet. The real indication that a prophet is false is if that person is trying to lead the people astray from God to follow after other gods.

A true prophet speaks the word of the Lord with the intention of bringing people closer to the Lord, causing them to walk more faithfully in His ways and turning them *away from bondage*.

God <<<─────────────────────────────Bondage

A false prophet speaks with the intention of causing people to follow after him or herself (leading the hearers into idolatry by following after a human) or causing people to follow after some other god. Either way, it leads people *away from the one true God*.

Bondage/idolatry <<<─────────────────God

For this reason, we must always pay close attention to what prophets are trying to lead us away from. Are they leading us toward evil and bondage but away from God? Are they trying to lead us closer to God or closer to themselves or another god? Their prophecies and teachings *must* line up with the whole counsel of the Scriptures. If the teachings do not match what God has already said and hold true to His character, they must be discarded! Nothing is higher or more advanced or the authority of the Scriptures (both Old and New Testament together). Nothing!

Do they encourage people to live godly or godless lives?

The entire chapter of Jeremiah 23 reveals God's thoughts about false prophets—*those who claim to speak for God, but care nothing for His ways or His people.*

> *Concerning the prophets: My heart is broken within me... because of the LORD and his holy words....Both prophet and priest are godless....Among the prophets of Samaria I saw this repulsive thing: They prophesied by Baal and led my people Israel astray. And among the prophets of Jerusalem I have seen something horrible: They commit adultery and live a lie. They strengthen the hands of evildoers, so that not one of them turns from their wickedness...* (Jeremiah 23:9, 11, 13–14).

The idea here is that if prophets are true and are really sent by Him, they will deliver messages that call the hearers to turn away from wickedness and toward following God. By contrast, because of false prophets, "*...ungodliness has spread throughout the land*" (Jer. 23:15). The false prophets were actually an evil influence upon God's people:

> *This is what the LORD Almighty says: "Do not listen to what the prophets are prophesying to you; they fill you with false*

> hopes. They speak visions from their own minds, not from the mouth of the LORD. They keep saying to those who despise me, 'The LORD says: You will have peace.' And to all who follow the stubbornness [or imagination] of their hearts they say, 'No harm will come to you'" (Jeremiah 23:16–17).

These false prophets were making the people worthless by soothing their consciences and telling them there were no consequences for their actions. They led the people to believe God did not mind them living in sin and not honoring His Word. They gave a false sense of peace. God wanted prophets who would stir the people to repent from sin, turn to Him, and begin to walk in His ways. (See 1 Corinthians 14:3.) Instead, the false prophets had prevented the people from hearing what God wanted to say to them. About them He said, *"I did not send these prophets, yet they have run with their message; I did not speak to them, yet they have prophesied"* (Jer. 23:21). This is a clear proof of false prophets—if their words give people license to live in sin (Jude 4).

Do they prophesy recklessly?

Reckless is defined as "a person or behavior that is too quick; not caring about danger to oneself or to others." About those who prophesied recklessly, God said:

> "Therefore," declares the LORD, "I am against the prophets who steal from one another words supposedly from me. Yes," declares the LORD, "I am against the prophets who wag their own tongues and yet declare, 'The LORD declares.' Indeed, I am against those who prophesy false dreams," declares the LORD. "They tell them and lead my people astray with their reckless lies, yet I did not send or appoint them. They do not benefit these people in the least," declares the LORD (Jeremiah 23:30–32).

God wants His prophets to be very careful and caring about their own character, as well as how they deal with His people.

Are they accountable to others?

False prophets tend to be loners who are unwilling to be accountable to others and do not like it when they are challenged or questioned (even in the most godly and gracious way). We must beware of those who act independently from authority and are not open to examination. This is a sign of stubbornness and rebellion, which will lead both the prophet and the hearers astray. True prophets will listen to God and be willing to receive His correction. (See Jeremiah 23:22.) By contrast, those who are false in ministry often wander around from place to place with no real connection to authority and no real place where their ministry can be proven and known.

The Epistle of Jude gives us a good look at the ministry of false prophets, showing us how these false prophets mirrored the false prophets in the Old Testament. Ideally, it should be read in one sitting to get the entire context. Here are some of the highlights:

> *…On the strength of their dreams these ungodly people pollute their own bodies, reject authority and heap abuse on celestial beings.… These people slander whatever they do not understand.… They have taken the way of Cain; they have rushed for profit into Balaam's error; they have been destroyed in Korah's rebellion.… They are wild waves of the sea, foaming up their shame; wandering stars, for whom blackest darkness has been reserved forever* (Jude 8, 10–11, 13).

> *These people are grumblers and faultfinders; they follow their own evil desires; they boast about themselves and flatter others for their own advantage.… They* [the apostles] *said to you, "In the last times there will be scoffers who will follow their own ungodly desires." These are the people who divide you, who follow mere natural instincts and do not have the Spirit* (Jude 16, 18–19).

In verse 11, these false prophets are specifically compared to Cain, Balaam, and Korah. Balaam, whose name means "devourer of the people" or "a conqueror of the people," is the subject of the next section. Cain and Korah are both examples of the result of a rebellious heart. Because *Cain* means "maker or fabricator, one who makes his own way," we can safely say *the way of Cain is self-will.* When Cain's offering was rejected, instead of receiving the correction and turning toward God, Cain became angry and depressed and eventually murdered his brother. He acted in self-will and was declared, by God, a fugitive for the rest of his life, wherever he went (see Gen. 4:11–12).

Self-will alienates people from God. When people walk in rebellion, they do not benefit from the protection of accountability to others and obedience to God, and as a result, they are easy prey for the enemy. When a prophet walks in self-will and rebellion, it should cause us to ask very serious questions.

By contrast, Paul described the right attitude all believers should have toward authority:

> *Now we ask you, brothers and sisters, to acknowledge those who work hard among you, who care for you in the Lord and who admonish you. Hold them in the highest regard in love because of their work. Live in peace with each other* (1 Thessalonians 5:12–13).

One of the best things we can do for ourselves and those around us is to develop an appreciation for authority. It is meant as a positive safeguard in our lives.

Lessons from the Life of Balaam

Now, let's look at the error of Balaam, a diviner-prophet who lived at Pethor, a city in Mesopotamia (see Deut. 23:4). He was most likely a Midianite (see Num. 31:8). Somehow, he possessed some knowledge of the true God and acknowledged that his powers were a gift from God.

In other words, *there was mixture in the use of Balaam's gift*. We need to be very careful of this ourselves. If we have been or are presently involved in anything cultic or occultic, we need to repent, renounce that area in our lives, and turn completely away from it. *If we want to be true prophetic people of God, we can have no mixture.* We need to dedicate ourselves completely to the service of God and not allow any other spiritual influences in our lives. (See *New Age Masquerade*, Jonathan Welton)

Balaam's fame was apparently widespread and accepted (see Num. 22:5, 7). When Balak, the king of Moab, entered into an agreement with the Midianites against the Israelites, they sent messengers to Balaam with a diviner's fee in their hands (see Num. 22:7; 1 Sam. 9:7–8). We don't know what was going through Balaam's mind at this point; at the very least, we can assume he may have felt good about himself. He may have felt flattered that this king had heard of him and had sent messengers to hear what he would tell them. *We need to guard our hearts so we are not willing to sell out when the opportunity comes along.*

Balaam was a diviner in a heathen nation, as well as one who heard from the one true God, so He was familiar with the idea of curses and blessings. Divination was the pagan counterpart of prophecy. It is the practice of obtaining hidden knowledge, especially regarding the future. A synonym we are familiar with is *fortune-telling*, and it comes in a variety of forms—palm reading, tarot cards, reading tea leaves, crystal balls, horoscopes, and Ouija boards. The source of divination is demonic power, while the source of genuine prophecy is the Spirit of God.

To understand what happened with Balaam, we must keep this mixture in mind. Otherwise, we will not understand why he would even consider cursing Israel (see Num. 22:6–7). Let's look at the story.

When Balak first summons Balaam, offering him all sorts of rewards for coming, Balaam's initial answer is absolutely wonderful. It is just the answer it should be. He says, no matter what the king offers him, *"I could not do anything great or small to go beyond the command of the LORD my God"* (Num. 22:18).

But then he adds, *"Now spend the night here so that I can find out what else the LORD will tell me"* (Num. 22:19). And so Balaam steps onto dangerous ground. We do not ever want to get involved in this type of behavior with the Lord. If He speaks something to us, we should say only that. We should not go back again and again to see if He will change His mind and say something different. If God did say something different to us, it would only mean trouble. It would mean He sees into our hearts and knows we want something different than His word. If He says something like, "Go ahead and go," we should beware!

Instead of fishing for the words we want, we must commit ourselves to be His faithful and willing servants and to speak only what He says to us, no matter what we could gain by saying something different. Later, Balaam says to Balak, *"'Well, I have come to you now....But I can't say whatever I please. I must speak only what God puts in my mouth'"* (Num. 22:38). May we all have the same resolve. Several times, Balak tried to convince Balaam to curse the Israelites, yet Balaam could not do it.

> *...Whatever he reveals to me I will tell you....Must I not speak what the LORD puts in my mouth?...Even if Balak gave me all the silver and gold in his palace, I could not do anything of my own accord, good or bad, to go beyond the command of the LORD—and I must say only what the LORD says* (Numbers 23:3, 12; 24:13).

Through all of these experiences, Balaam's words sounded right, but his heart must have been somewhere else. That is why he was willing to go so many places with Balak and repeatedly ask if God would curse Israel. The apostle Peter revealed the reality of Balaam's heart when he wrote:

> *They have left the straight way and wandered off to follow the way of Balaam son of Bezer, who loved the wages of wickedness. But he was rebuked for his wrongdoing by a donkey—an animal without speech—who spoke with a human voice and restrained the prophet's madness* (2 Peter 2:15–16).

Balaam loved the riches, and because of them, he was willing to go with Balak's messengers. This is a warning to us. *We must be very wary of going beyond what God is really saying for the sake of riches and honor!* His love of riches led to his downfall. And eventually he died at the hand of the Israelites for practicing divination (see Josh. 13:22).

In the life of Balaam we see the reality that each one of us, if we do not guard our hearts from sins like greed and pride, can be led away into deception. Many of those who have become false prophets did not set out to be false prophets. Instead, the weaknesses in their character allowed them to be slowly deluded and to cause great harm to others. Not only are we responsible to test and discern the words and character of prophets, in order to identify those who may be false, but we also must keep our hearts always open before God and allow Him to search us for any false ways or beliefs. This is the truest way to avoid false prophecy.

eleven

The Character of the Servant of the Lord

Prophecy is not just about accuracy but also about delivery. As mentioned in Chapter 3, on God's heart of restoration, it is not enough to just say the words. The heart of God must also come through the message. Even in human relationships, a messenger between two parties must deliver the message with the same attitude and heart as the sender; otherwise, the meaning of the message can be completely lost or, at minimum, distorted.

Ideally, people ministering prophetically will embody:

Gifting + Humility + Character

We need all three traits to minister maturely and in a way that will bless people and bring glory to God. The apostle James highlights for us what true Christian character should look like:

> *Who is wise and understanding among you? Let them show it by their good life, by deeds done in the humility that comes from wisdom. But if you harbor bitter envy and selfish ambition in your hearts, do not boast about it or deny the truth. Such "wisdom" does not come down from heaven but is earthly, unspiritual, demonic. For where you have envy*

> *and selfish ambition, there you find disorder and every evil practice. But the wisdom that comes from heaven is first of all pure; then peace-loving, considerate, submissive, full of mercy and good fruit, impartial and sincere* (James 3:13–17).

We really do show our fitness for ministry through our "good life" and the proof of humility and wisdom. Those ministering in the Church should not only have gifts of the Spirit but also the fruit of the Spirit: *"But the fruit of the Spirit is love, joy, peace, forbearance, kindness, goodness, faithfulness, gentleness and self-control…* (Gal. 5:22–23). The apostle Peter also emphasized the importance of character, telling believers to use their gifts for the benefit of others and not for selfish purposes:

> *Each of you should use whatever gift you have received to serve others, as faithful stewards of God's grace in its various forms. If anyone speaks, they should do so as one who speaks the very words of God. If anyone serves, they should do so with the strength God provides, so that in all things God may be praised through Jesus Christ…* (1 Peter 4:10–11).

Here we see the proof of godly ministry—it is done according to God's strength, and He receives all the glory for it. In a nutshell, Peter says, ministry means being a servant, just like Jesus was a servant, and stewarding well the gifts He has given us. This was exactly the lesson Peter had to learn from Jesus before He was ready to lead the early Church: *"The greatest among you will be your servant. For those who exalt themselves will be humbled, and those who humble themselves will be exalted"* (Matt. 23:11; see Luke 22:24–27). Jesus set the example for servant leadership, and we are to be like Him:

> *God was reconciling the world to himself in Christ, not counting people's sins against them. And he has committed to us the message of reconciliation. We are therefore Christ's ambassadors, as though God were making his appeal through us. We implore you on Christ's behalf: Be reconciled to God* (2 Corinthians 5:19–20).

Our goal is to be clear channels for the personality of Jesus Christ to anyone around us. Revelation 19:10 says, *"...for the testimony of Jesus is the spirit of prophecy"* (NKJV). This has a dual meaning: First, the truth revealed by Jesus is the inspiration of all prophecy. Second, it is the truth concerning Jesus that inspires all prophecy. As people who minister prophetically, the prophetic words we give must always be inspired by Jesus and point people toward Him. In a very real sense, prophetic ministry should give people an encounter with the living Christ. For this to happen, God must deal with our inner issues and character weaknesses. This is what the writer of Hebrews was talking about when he wrote that we should *"see to it that no one falls short of the grace of God and that no bitter root grows up to cause trouble and defile many"* (Heb. 12:15). We would never intentionally harm or destroy people, but if we are not aware of our inner lives and problems (and allowing God to change them), we will end up unintentionally harming others. If we have toxic areas in our lives, we can end up distributing that toxicity to those in our sphere of influence. This is very serious. It is why we must care so much about growing in character and allowing God to pinpoint areas of sin or dysfunction in our lives. Most of all, it shows the importance of walking in true, biblical love, which is the definition of Christian character.

First Corinthians 13, the love chapter, has been overused in Valentine's Day cards and at weddings, to the point of cliché. In that process, we have lost sight of what Paul really meant when he wrote this to the Corinthian believers. Let's consider why Paul inserted this chapter on love in the midst of his discussion of the gifts of the Holy Spirit in chapters 12 and 14. Paul was a highly educated man, and his thoughts flowed coherently. He did not carelessly go down rabbit trails of thought. When he shared something, he had a clear point, a reason for saying what he said. That point in First Corinthians 13 becomes clear when we consider the importance of Christian character in the operation of the gifts of the Spirit.

Paul was telling the Corinthian believers that God was not interested in having them use the gifts to impress others; he wanted them to know

God cares about how His gifts are used and the impact they have on others. He wanted everything done from love and in love. God went so far as to say, through Paul, that all the great and glorious things believers do in His name are worthless in His eyes if they are not motivated by true, Christ-like love. Clearly, love is a pretty big deal. So Paul wrote out exactly what this love acts like. It is the definition of maturity, the goal we should all reach for in all areas of our lives, especially when ministering in the gifts of the Spirit.

Following is my own paraphrase of First Corinthians 13:

> Even if I speak in every human and angelic language, if I do not have love in my heart, I am only making a lot of noise.
>
> Even if I speak God's word and know all sorts of sacred secrets and hidden truths and even if I have such absolute faith that I can move mountains from their place, if I don't have love, *my actions are worth nothing.*
>
> Even if I distribute all I possess to those who are in need around me or if I am burned alive for preaching the gospel, if I do not have love, *it is of no value.*
>
> This is what this love that I speak of looks like:
>
> 1. It is slow to lose patience, and it always looks for a way to be constructive.
>
> 2. It is not anxious to impress others, it does not envy others, and it does not make a practice of being boastful.
>
> 3. It is not arrogant, and it is not puffed up with ideas of how important it is.
>
> 4. It is not rude or unmannerly.
>
> 5. It does not insist on its own way or spend its energy on selfish ambitions.

6. Love is not quick to take offense.

7. It is not irritable or resentful.

8. It does not gloat over other people's sins.

9. It is never glad when others go wrong.

10. It is always glad when the truth prevails.

11. Love is slow to expose other peoples' faults and failures.

12. It is always eager to believe the best.

13. It bears up under anything.

14. There is nothing that love cannot face.

15. Love continues to hope under all circumstances, and it endures without limit.

16. Love gives us the power to endure everything.

Love will never come to an end, because God is love.

This kind of love is the key to Christian character and the maturity needed to use the gifts of the Spirit in a way that will bless people and honor God. Without it, we cannot possibly hope to succeed in speaking God's word on His behalf and conveying His heart to people.

We see this reality in the news we hear, from time to time, of well-known ministers falling into sin. We wonder how this sort of thing could happen. Often, we felt quite sure this minister lived with integrity and was upright. The revelation of significant sin took us by surprise and possibly caused us to question what the minister stood for, as well as the minister's beliefs, ministries, and even God. It may not cause us to fall or turn away from God, but it does cause shaking and questioning. The larger the influence of the person's ministry, the larger the shaking and damage will be if that person falls. It brings shame and dishonor to that person and ministry, and it dishonors God in the eyes of the world. It also introduces a problem into the lives of both weak and strong believers. The stronger ones experience momentary sadness and disbelief in their hearts, but the weaker ones may experience a very lasting devastation in their lives.

How does this happen? The answer is simple. People do not start out in ministry with the intention of failing in front of the world. In the beginning, they were most likely motivated by a desire to obey God and serve those around them. However, if an area of personal unhealthiness is not addressed in their lives—perhaps a desire for a certain thing or a need in a particular area—that area of dysfunction will color their entire lives. It will come out in one way or another. It is like clothing dye. To some degree, it will affect whatever it comes in contact with. In the end, it can be the downfall of the person and ministry. Most often, the family of that person suffers the most.

I call these areas of personal unhealthiness that are not dealt with *hooks and openings*. I use *hooks* because they provide something the enemy of our lives can hook us with, and suddenly, without planning it, we find ourselves going in a certain direction. He is able to drag us around. *Openings* give the same idea. They provide an entrance through which satan can come into our lives and wreak havoc. Since these areas are not dealt with and under the lordship of Jesus Christ, they are open and available for him to work with. And he comes only to kill, steal, and destroy (see John 10:10). For this reason, we must all, day-by-day, ask the Lord to search our hearts. We must commit ourselves to always being willing to look at anything He may present to us, any area needing greater conformity to His image. It is a lot less painful to take care of an issue while it is still small and private than it is to have to deal with it while the world watches. We don't want to live in fear of failure, of course, yet it is wisdom to seriously consider the ramifications of operating in the gifts of the Spirit without continually inviting and allowing God to increase our character and our manifestation of the love of God in all things.

This should be our goal in prophecy and in ministry, after all. And when our hearts are toward God and toward His people and we are embracing the way of humility and growth, we will be ones whom God can use mightily to edify, exhort, and comfort His body.

Conclusion

Hopefully by now you have a good grasp on what biblical prophecy looks like (as well as what it doesn't look like), and you are ready to embrace this gift of God to His Church. The truth of Scripture and a revelation of God's heart for restoration are the framework that allow for healthy, biblical prophecy. When we keep these in our hearts and minds, they will keep us safe as we explore the amazing and exciting world of the prophetic. God loves to speak to His people, and He wants us to feel at home in the spirit realm, so He has provided us with the framework we need to protect ourselves from deception and from false prophets.

We hope this book has encouraged you to pursue the spiritual gifts—and especially prophecy (see 1 Cor. 14:1). Here we have only scratched the surface of what God has made available to each one of us, and we hope the foundation we've presented here will be a stepping stone that will help you discover more of your spiritual inheritance in Christ in a biblical way.

> *Each of you should use whatever gift you have received to serve others, as faithful stewards of God's grace in its various forms. If anyone speaks, they should do so as one who speaks the very words of God. If anyone serves, they should do so with the strength God provides, so that in all things God may be praised through Jesus Christ. To him be the glory and the power forever and ever. Amen* (1 Peter 4:10–11).

Appendix
Forming Prophetic Teams

In the year 2000, we met with our pastor to discuss how we could help the gifts of the Spirit flow in our local church. We shared our hearts with him, and he encouraged us to go ahead and organize prophetic teams. So we set out to create as foolproof, safe, and comfortable of a setting as possible, where people could learn and grow in hearing and delivering words of prophecy. Starting with just twelve people, we decided to form four teams of three. We designated four people as team leaders, with two others as team members. This created a measure of accountability on the teams, and the leader was empowered to oversee and carry out the various guidelines. After prophetic ministry, we would meet as a group to hear how it had gone and any issues that may have come up. It was an excellent learning tool for all of us.

During that time, we also wrote the training manual that was the beginning of this book. This helped us to all be on the same page and work more efficiently together. We wanted to make this group a safe place for our team members to learn and practicing, and we wanted them to learn how to make those coming for ministry feel safe and comfortable, too.

The prophetic ministry on a Sunday morning at our church looked like this. After the service, people who wanted prophetic ministry would come to the designated area. Cards with numbers on them were handed out to people in the order they arrived. We tried, as much as possible to give preferential treatment to the elderly, disabled, and parents of small children, in order to diminish their time waiting in line. We always asked those in the front of the line if that was OK, and almost always people were glad to let these others go ahead of them.

Personal ministry generally took ten to fifteen minutes. We stressed the importance of no visiting before, during, or after prophetic ministry. Often people wanted to ask the teams to explain what their words meant, and if they weren't careful, they would get drawn into conversation. We also stressed the importance of avoiding pet-doctrines in our prophecies. In other words, if someone sells vitamins or believes in green drinks for health, one should not include anything about vitamins or green drinks in the prophecy. Also, strong opinions on child rearing or marriage relationships should not be mentioned in prophetic words. Some people are prone to molding so-called prophecies around these thoughts, but this is not true prophecy. of the purpose of prophecy is always hearing and speaking forth the word of the Lord, not our own ideas and opinions.

During prophetic ministry, we always had what we called a "prophetic box" handy, with tissues, breath mints, fresh batteries, pens, and name tags for team members. We also kept it stocked with extra cassette tapes and recorders, because we recorded every prophecy in order to keep the prophetic ministry safe and accountable. Now, tape recorders have been replaced by more modern technology, but the value of recording prophecies is the same. In fact, thanks to the advent of smart phones, it has never been easier.

When people came for ministry, we would ask them not to share anything with us except their name (into the recorder). The team leader would then ask participants if it was OK for the team to lay hands on them. (This is important because one never knows what others have experienced in their lifetime.) After this, the team members would each say their names into the recorder, thereby taking full responsibility for the words they were delivering.

The team members would then take turns sharing whatever God was speaking to them. Usually, one person's words, thoughts, pictures, Bible verses, songs (whatever that person happened to get) would build on each other. As that person shared, it would give a fuller, more understandable picture and would be a confirming word to the person being ministered to. After the team finished ministering, one would close in prayer and bless the person. They then gave the person an evaluation card and asked that person, if willing, to fill it out and place it in the suggestion box on the way out of the sanctuary. That way, the feedback was private and went directly to the pastors, not us. We wanted to be as accountable as possible and to give prophecy a good reputation. The evaluation cards were then read by the church leaders, who shared a summary of them with us. This ended up being a real source of encouragement to all of us who served together in this ministry.

The prophetic ministry soon became a real blessing to the church and was available every Sunday morning after both church services. In order to continue that schedule on a long-term basis, we realized we needed to train more team members. Because it is easier to train people to prophesy than to put character into them, we looked for people who were already demonstrating servanthood in other areas and who had a good understanding of the Bible. We would look for faithfulness, caring for people, willingness to be humble and learn, and so forth. We made of list of these people and sent it to the pastors, who looked over the list and approved those we could invite for training. When people were not approved, it was because of difficulties they were having at home, had issues in their lives that the pastors knew about and we didn't, or were already over-committed. We then invited those on the approved list to receive training for prophetic ministry. Nearly everyone we invited came to the trainings, and most of them were added to the teams. This process continued for several years until we had over thirty people available to help on Sunday mornings or to travel with us to college campuses and other churches.

Because of our experiences with prophecy in the 1970s, we were extremely cautious about what was being said and how things were being done. We did not want people to cross lines and harm anyone with so-called prophecies. So we set up guidelines to help those who were just learning and practicing.

Prophetic Team Guidelines

The following is a list of general guidelines that are to be followed during the prophetic ministry times:

1. Limit the expression of prophetic ministry to words of encouragement, exhortation, and comfort (see 1 Cor. 14:3). This is not a time for rebuke, correction, or specific direction in peoples' lives.

2. Remember that prophetic ministry is a combination of the message *and* the heart of God. Therefore, do not prophesy negatively. God reveals problems and strongholds because He wants to bring deliverance and freedom, not condemnation. Approach everything with humility.

3. Do not prophesy the problem but instead prophesy the promise and the potential for change from God. If God shows you someone has struggled with depression, prophesy the joy, liberty, and freedom God wants to release to that person.

4. The following are examples of things not to prophesy: Do not prophesy that a person should or should not marry a particular person; do not prophesy that a person should or should not have a baby; do not prophesy that a person should or should not divorce; do not prophesy that a person should give money to a certain organization; do

not prophesy that a person should move geographically; do not prophesy that a person should join your church; do not prophesy that a person is one of the five-fold ministry gifts; do not prophesy pregnancy or the sex of an unborn child; do not prophesy anything that contradicts the Scriptures; and do not prophesy healing, especially in the case of terminal illness.

5. Do not give counsel during these sessions. We are here to prophesy, not counsel.

6. Remember that the spirit of the person prophesying is subject to him or her. That means, you are able to follow these guidelines. If you believe you have received revelation in one of these areas, feel free to talk it over with one of the pastors or to call the prophetic ministry leaders, but do not share with the person during the designated ministry time. We are all learning, and we only prophesy in part and understand in part, so be open and flexible. This is not *your* word, so don't take personal ownership of it. Hold it loosely and allow it to be tested. If you are hearing correctly, it will stand the test. Character + Humility + Gifting = a good vessel for prophecy.

7. If the Spirit is not saying anything, do not say anything.

These guidelines helped minimize misuse of prophetic ministry in our church of eight hundred to one thousand adults, where on any given Sunday we could encounter people from a great variety of backgrounds. One experience we had quickly taught us to always ask a couple who comes for prophecy whether they are married. By assuming they are married and prophesying over them together, it sends a message of approval and suggests God is in favor of the relationship. Obviously, we do not want them to make such an important decision based on a prophesy. For this reason, we told our team members not to prophesy over unmarried couples together, even if they were getting married the same day. We did not want them to claim that through prophecy God had affirmed the marriage.

One Sunday morning a couple came for prophecy, holding hands and looking all sweet. Our team leader asked if they were married, they said yes, and the ministry began. It was all very positive and encouraging. Later in the afternoon, we received a phone call at home from the sister of the lady, asking why our people had approved of her married sister having a relationship with a married man. I asked her if I could call the team leader and find out exactly what had happened. When I did, the team leader told me none of the prophecies had actually mentioned anything about the relationship, though they had been encouraging. However, the couple had taken all of it as God's blessing on the relationship. Turns out, when the team asked if the couple was married, and they answered yes, they failed to mention they were not married *to each other!*

What a teachable moment. We learned that when two people came together we should not assume they were married. Instead, we should ask them directly if they are married *to each other*. If they are not, then we prophesy over them individually. In the case of this couple, we called them back and shared our mistake, as well as the fact that God was not putting His blessing on their relationship. The man was counseled to return to his wife and try to work out his marriage problems, and the woman was counseled to release the man to do so. Prophecy never trumps biblical principles, and God will not contradict Himself.

We used to recommend that if one of the team members knew the person coming for prophecy, they should switch places and work on another team, just so the person would not feel uncomfortable. Also, if one of the team members had a problem or an offense with the person coming for ministry, excuse themselves, step away, and deal with their attitudes before trying to prophesy over them. If they could not get things straight within themselves right then, switch with another team, continue; and after church, go to the person and get things straightened out. God can use us even when we are not in a perfect state because He wants to bless the other person. He might not be thrilled with our attitude, but He still wants to speak to the person, and you're the vessel He has at the moment!

Activations

Throughout the prophetic training, we used some of the following activations as ice-breakers for those who have had little or no experience with the prophetic.

Activation #1

Choose a volunteer from the class who is willing to come to the front and allow people to practice receiving and delivering words of prophecy to him or her. Explain to the class that everyone is going to be quiet for a little while and ask the Lord what He would like to say to this particular person. Instead of just saying the thoughts, the students are going to search around the room for something they can use as a prop to help illustrate what they have to share.

Afterward, be sure to thank the volunteer and ask if he or she was encouraged, exhorted, and comforted. The person doesn't have to give specific details, but as long as the person can say yes to one or all of these, prophesy has happened properly. This is always a fun activation because it gets people thinking, gives them a chance to move around, and pushes them to step out of their comfort zones just a little bit.

Activation #2

Ask for a volunteer and have that person come to the front. Gestures are similar props (in Activation #1), except they use motions to illustrate the message. For example, you might use your hands to brush something off the person's shoulders that has been weighing that person down. You might blow in the person's direction to say the Lord is breathing new life or is blowing away the old and bringing in the new. The Spirit may reveal that the person has been "stabbed in the back by a friend," and you could gesture as if you were pulling out the knife from the center of that person's back. Placing your hands in a gesture, as if making a crown or cap to fit over a person's head, could speak of God's desire to renew that person's mind or give new revelation and understanding of the Scriptures.

Activation #3

Again, ask for a volunteer. Then ask the class to be quiet and ask the Lord to give them something that would encourage, stimulate to action, or comfort the person. This time they want just one word or one picture or one color—but just one. After a few minutes, ask people to call out what they have, one at a time so you can write them down on a white board. Make a list of about ten things. Then, ask the same people (and any others who now want to enter in) to broaden this one-word list. If a person saw a watch, ask whether it gold or silver. Was it a wind-up or a digital? Did it have a particular time on it? Usually, the prophetic word will unfold during this process. The person will begin to see or hear more, as will others who may just have been sitting by before. If a person sees a flower, ask what kind it is. What color is it? What does it smell like? Is it growing, or has it been picked? Is it alone, or is it being put into a bouquet? Do this with each word that was part of the initial list, getting the students to expand what they are seeing, hearing, feeling, smelling, and tasting.

Activation #4

Have the entire class stand up and form two lines parallel to each other. Have them turn their backs to each other and take two steps to the right or the left so they are back-to-back with someone, but they don't know who it is. Take just a few minutes for them to quiet themselves. Then ask them to turn around and share what they have with the person they are now facing. After a set time, have them turn back-to-back again and repeat the activation. This stretches the students because they do not have any idea who is behind them.

Activation #5

Have a volunteer come to the front. Invite people to speak out (one at a time) what they are receiving for the volunteer. Allow a number of people to participate; don't limit this to just two or three. Then ask the volunteer to give some encouraging feedback to the class (it doesn't have to be specific).

Activation #6

Sometimes we ask the class to get prophetic words for us since they don't know us or what is happening in our lives. You can do this as the leader of the group, or you can choose someone you are thinking of who is not there. However, you would need to know the person quite well so you can know if the students are getting their words correct or not. Then you can give them feedback on what they got right. The more you can encourage the participants, the better.

Endnotes

1. Donald Gee, *Concerning Spiritual Gifts* (Gospel Publishing House, 1972).

2. *Strong's Exhaustive Concordance*, s.v. "covet"; Greek #2206.

3. Steve Thompson, *You May All Prophesy: Practical Guidelines for Prophetic Ministry* (MorningStar, 2005), 11.

4. *The New Bible Dictionary*.

ADDITIONAL MATERIAL BY JONATHAN WELTON

Eyes of Honor: Training for Purity and Righteousness
by Jonathan Welton

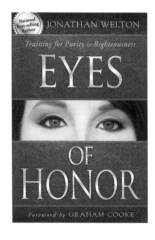

After struggling with sexual temptation for years, author Jonathan Welton devoted himself to finding a way to be completely free from sexual sin. He read books, attended 12-step groups, and participated in counseling—with no success.

Spurred on by countless friends and acquaintances who shared a similar broken struggle and longed for freedom, the author searched Scripture. There he found the answer, which he shares with you in a compassionate, nonjudgmental way.

Eyes of Honor helps you understand how to live a life of purity by realizing:
- Your personal identity
- How to view the opposite sex correctly
- Who your enemies are

Eyes of Honor is honest and refreshing, offering hope and complete freedom and deliverance from sexual sin. Jesus' sacrifice on the cross and your salvation guarantee rescue from the appetite of sin. Your true identity empowers you to stop agreeing with lies of the enemy that ensnare you.

"This book is stunningly profound. He got my attention and kept it."   ~ **Dr. John Roddam**, St. Luke's Episcopal

"Jonathan has written one of the best books on being free from bondage by dealing with the root issues of sin. I highly recommend reading this book.
              ~ **Dr. Che Ahn,** Chancellor Wagner Leadership

ADDITIONAL MATERIAL BY JONATHAN WELTON

Raptureless: An Optimistic Guide to the End of the World by Jonathan Welton

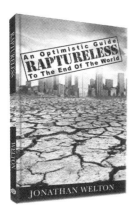

What others have said...

Jonathan Welton is a voice to the rising Church. We need his teaching gift stirring the Body of Christ to action. Here in *Raptureless*, Jonathan has revealed his scholarship and ability to communicate on issues pertinent to today's Church.

~ **Harold Eberle**

Jonathan Welton has taken a bold step in confronting one of the greatest "sacred cows" of our day: end-time theology! The fear created by the expectation of a coming antichrist and a great tribulation are keeping many believers in bondage. Many believe that defeat is the future destiny of the Church. In his easy-to-read presentation, Jonathan dismantles many of the popular ideas in the Church about the end times.

~ **Joe McIntyre**

Jonathan Welton's new book, *Raptureless*, is a must read. His insights on various passages of Scripture are powerfully presented. In addition, Jonathan provides fresh historical background for a number of the historical sources that he has quoted, such as Flavius Josephus.   ~ **George Kouri**

Book TWO in the series

Book ONE: The Advancing Kingdom

Book TWO: Raptureless

Book THREE: The Art of Revelation

ADDITIONAL MATERIAL BY JONATHAN WELTON

The School of the Seers by Jonathan Welton

Your how-to guide into the spirit realm!

The School of the Seers is more than a compilation of anecdotal stories. It is the how-to guide for seeing into the spirit realm.

The fresh, profound, and new concepts taught in this book take a mystical subject (seers and the spirit realm) and make them relevant for everyday life.This book takes some of the difficult material presented in other seer books and makes it easy to understand, removes the spookiness, and provides practical application of a dimension that is biblically based and scripturally sound. Get ready to enter the world of a seer! In this groundbreaking and revelatory book, Jonathan Welton describes his unique journey in which God opened his spiritual eyes. He shares how you too can activate this gift in your life.

Discover the keys from Scripture that will help you:

- See with your spiritual eyes.
- Use the four keys to greater experiences.
- Recognize what may be hindering your discernment.
- Learn about the four spirits.
- Access divine secrets and steward heavenly revelation.
- Learn how to really worship in Spirit and in Truth.
- Understand meditation, impartation, and so much more…

ADDITIONAL MATERIAL BY JONATHAN WELTON

Normal Christianity: If Jesus is Normal, what is the Church? by Jonathan Welton

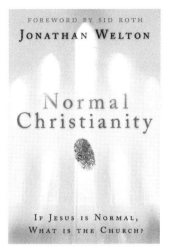

Jesus and the Book of Acts are the standard of *Normal Christianity*.

Remember the fad a few years ago when people wore bracelets reminding them, What Would Jesus Do? Christians state that Jesus is the example of how to live, yet this has been limited in many cases to how we view our moral character. When Christians tell me they want to live like Jesus, I like to ask if they have multiplied food, healed the sick, walked on water, raised the dead, paid their taxes with fish money, calmed storms, and so forth. I typically receive bewildered looks, but that is what it is like to live like Jesus!

Perhaps we are ignoring a large portion of what living like Jesus really includes. Many Christians believe they can live like Jesus without ever operating in the supernatural. After reading in the Bible about all the miracles He performed, does that sound right to you? (Excerpt from book)

What others have said

I believe before Jesus returns there will be two churches. One will be religious, and the other will be normal. This book of Jonathan Welton's will help restore your childlike faith, and you will become normal!

~ **Sid Roth,** Host of It's Supernatural! Television Program

Aurora Writing & Editing Services

AMY CALKINS,
WRITER & EDITOR

Amy Calkins is not only a dear friend, but also a tremendous writer and editor. I have had the pleasure of working with her on four of my books, and she is a gift of God. I would strongly urge anyone to work with her; she will help you take your writing to a whole new level.

—Jonathan Welton

Writing an effective and influential book is not as simple as typing up your ideas in a book-length document and sending it off to the printer. Getting a book into print is easier now than it's ever been due to the growth of low-cost self-publishing and the powerful communication tools available through the internet. Yet the ability to craft a well-written and effective book still takes time and expertise. That's where Aurora comes in. Let us help you craft your ideas and message into a form that will have the ability to influence and inspire. Whether through ghostwriting, copyediting, or proofreading, we want to help your book succeed. For more information on what these services entail, as well as endorsements from authors we've worked with, visit aurora-pub.com.

WWW.AURORA-PUB.COM